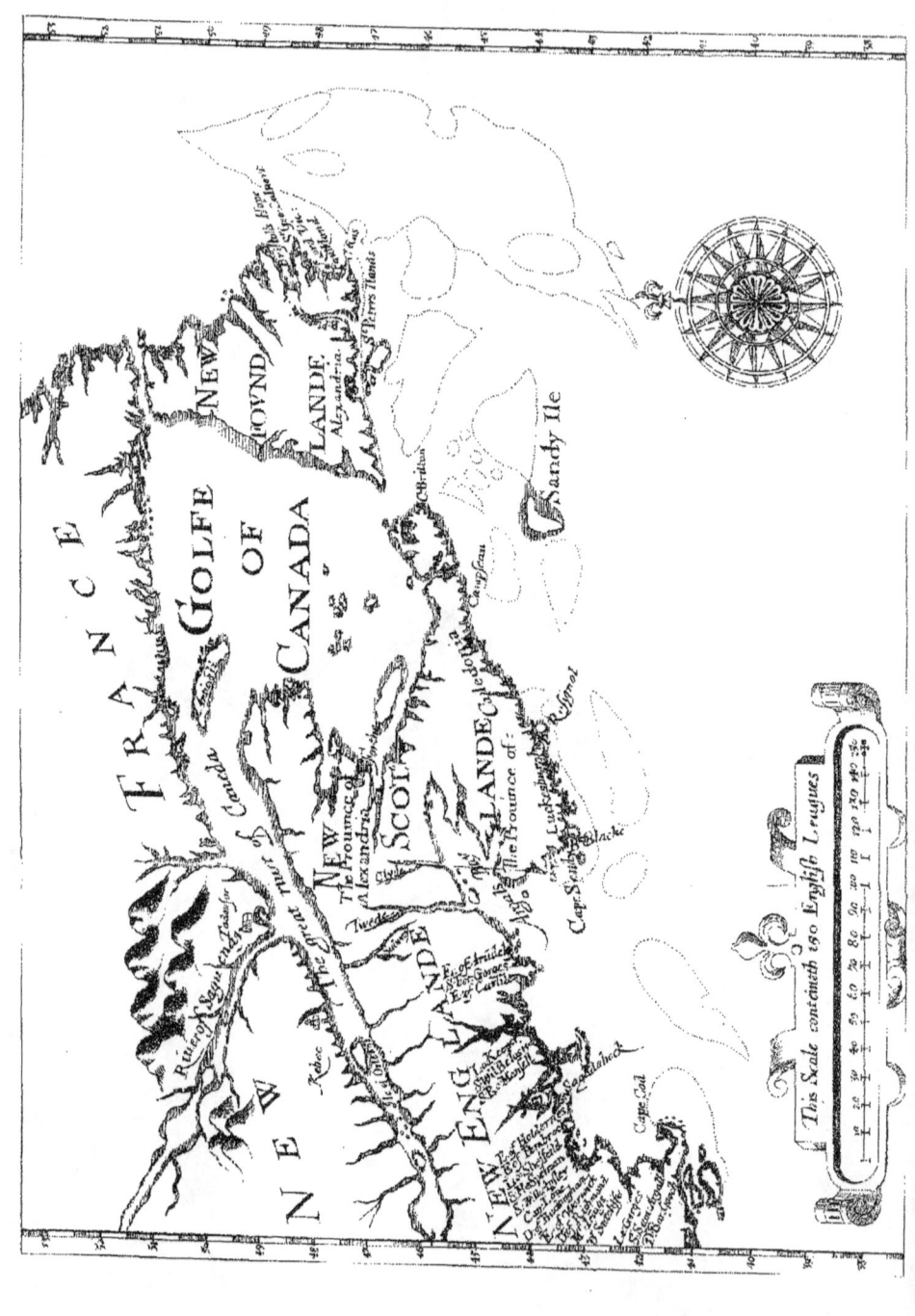

RESULT

OF SOME

RESEARCHES

AMONG THE BRITISH ARCHIVES

FOR INFORMATION RELATIVE TO

THE FOUNDERS OF NEW ENGLAND:

MADE IN THE YEARS 1858, 1859 AND 1860.

ORIGINALLY COLLECTED FOR AND PUBLISHED IN THE NEW ENGLAND HISTORICAL AND
GENEALOGICAL REGISTER; AND NOW CORRECTED AND ENLARGED.

BY SAMUEL G. DRAKE,

LATE PRESIDENT OF THE NEW ENGLAND HISTORIC-GENEALOGICAL SOCIETY.

BOSTON:
PUBLISHED AT THE OFFICE OF
THE NEW ENG. HIST. AND GEN. REGISTER,
No. 13, BROMFIELD STREET.
1860.

Notice

In many older books, foxing (or discoloration) occurs and, in some instances, print lightens with wear and age. Reprinted books, such as this, often duplicate these flaws, notwithstanding efforts to reduce or eliminate them. The pages of this reprint have been digitally enhanced and, where possible, the flaws eliminated in order to provide clarity of content and a pleasant reading experience.

Result of Some Researches Among the British Archives
For Information Relative to
The Founders of New England:
Made in the Years 1858, 1859, and 1860

Originally published
Boston
1860

Reprinted by:

Janaway Publishing, Inc.
732 Kelsey Ct.
Santa Maria, California 93454
(805) 925-1038
www.JanawayPublishing.com

2010

ISBN10: 159641202X
ISBN13: 9781596412026

Made in the United States of America

TO

JOHN BARSTOW, ESQUIRE,

OF PROVIDENCE,

ONE OF

THE VICE PRESIDENTS

OF

THE NEW ENGLAND HISTORIC-GENEALOGICAL SOCIETY,

THIS VOLUME,

DEVOTED TO THE FOUNDERS OF NEW ENGLAND,

IS DEDICATED,

AS A TRIBUTE JUSTLY DUE FOR HIS INTEREST IN, AND ENCOURAGEMENT OF,

THE OBJECTS OF THAT SOCIETY,

BY HIS ASSOCIATE AND FRIEND,

THE EDITOR.

INTRODUCTION.

THIS designation is not intended to convey the idea that all the names of the founders of New England are contained in the following collection; while all such as emigrated with a view to a permanent residence during the first years of settlement, or previous to King Philip's war, well deserve to be numbered among the FOUNDERS OF NEW ENGLAND; and this, it is thought, sufficiently justifies the designation.

Nearly the whole of the following work was prepared, (independent of any copy,) during a residence in the British Metropolis, in the years 1858, 1859, and 1860. This statement is made that the reader may understand certain expressions; as, in speaking of New England, *that* country is mentioned, and of England, as *this* country, &c. In all other respects it is presumed that the necessary explanations will be found in foot notes, or within brackets.

I had intended to accompany the work with some *indications* to antiquaries and genealogists, as to certain localities and means most likely to aid them in their investigations in England. But such a labor would require the compass of a work itself.

Such a work would not interfere at all with the valuable publication of Mr. Sims, of the British Museum, for what I had intended to do was to indicate the English localities of as many of our early New England emigrants as my collection of materials would enable me. So that, for example, a given name might be sought in a locality where it was known to have existed at the period of emigration. The importance of such a work will readily be perceived, but its accomplishment cannot be so readily performed. I shall therefore close these introductory observations with a few desultory remarks concerning researches, records, &c.

Whoever goes to England expecting to find the genealogy of any particular English family settled in New England at an early day, is pretty sure, in at least nine cases out of ten, to meet with disappointment. He will, if he looks for the names of Smith, Brown, Jones, &c., find enough of them; but, to connect an ancestor bearing one of these names, with the ancestor of a New England family of the same surname, is a desideratum of much uncertainty. The reason of this uncertainty is easily explained. In the first place, persons who emigrate are not often possessors of real estate, and hence deeds and wills seldom furnish indications referable to them. They leave no deeds or wills in the father land by which they can be traced. In the next place, very few emigrants from England were landholders, for the reason that for ages little or no land has been for sale in quantities within the reach of persons of moderate estates. William the Conqueror parcelled out all England to, comparatively, a few of his followers, and the dependents of those followers improved the vast domains by a sort of tenure, which in time grew into the leasing system, by which system, probably, above seven eighths of the present inhabitants of that country hold their places of residence and business.

As though the estates thus awarded were not sufficiently extensive, it not unfrequently happened that an estate, and sometimes several estates, reverted to the crown by confiscation; and such were conferred on some favorite already in possession of extensive domains; while the crown was careful to serve itself plentifully in the first place. The revenue to the sovereign from the crown lands, even to this day, are by no means inconsiderable.

It sometimes fell out that persons came into possession of lands by heirship, where the prospect originally appeared so small as to be scarcely worthy of attention. But such cases were always rare.

Hence, for the descendant of a New England emigrant to find his ancestor among the nobility or landed gentry of the period of the emigration, is about as certain as it would be to find him among those classes of the present day!

As the great body of emigrants to New England took no pains to transmit to their descendants any account of their ancestors, or even the places whence they came, it is pretty evident they had nothing to expect from the one, or any special regard for the other. Where parish registers have been preserved, some data are often found and made available in New England pedigrees. But they seldom indicate any connection with the so called higher classes.

Classes were and are very distinct in England. The class of servants, the class of tradespeople, the class of mechanics, &c., have continued for a long period of time. They mixed very little with those above them. Few of these ever became landholders, and few ever thought of a pedigree. Pedigrees may be said to have originated with the immediate descendants of the possessors of landed estates. They grew out of a necessity. Thus Genealogy became a *science*, and the learned pursued it as a useful and necessary branch of knowledge; and as such it is generally pursued in this country, especially in New England. There are those who pursue it with a notion that they are heirs to a great estate in England, left by some unknown ancestor. They may thus add something to the science of genealogy, and enlarge their own knowledge, while they will find no necessity to enlarge their pockets.

An exceedingly amusing article might be written upon the efforts of numerous families and individuals to obtain property left by their ancestors in England, at some remote period, as they imagine. And it may be pretty safely asserted, that the majority of such fortune hunters cannot trace their own line to their emigrant ancestor! Indeed, some have started for England to obtain, as descendants, the property of an individual who never had any descendants; and this knowledge was within the reach of everybody on this side of the Atlantic! But to take up space with these remarks may be considered unnecessary by the intelligent reader.

The sources of information in England have been greatly improved within the present century. Many restrictions upon the public records have been thrown off, and an immense amount of original papers, public and private, have found, and are daily finding, their way into that vast and well arranged and well conducted repository—the British Museum. And though it may be said that much remains to be done, in laying open, collecting, and arranging the records of England, at the same time it may be observed, that the extent and magnitude of what has already been done, could it be fully stated, would surpass belief.

It is high time the British government placed the ancient wills of the realm in a position to be consulted and used; especially those in the keeping of the Prerogative Court of Canterbury. This is the most extensive collection in the kingdom, and ought to be free for all genealogical and other literary uses. Yet the keepers of this repository are obliged to subject all applicants to heavy fees. In the beginning of 1859, an attempt was made to open Doctors' Commons to literary inquirers. A petition to Parliament was drawn up, ably setting forth the advantages which would accrue to the literary public by making that depository as free as the British Museum. This was headed by Lord Macaulay and other eminent gentlemen; but Parliament thought the time had not come for such liberality in Doctors' Commons, and thus the matter rests, and may possibly rest till another Sir Nicholas Harris Nicolas shall appear.

And here I may be pardoned for referring to that preëminent antiquary, who was cut off in the prime of life, while successfully advocating the cause of a free use of the public records, " whenever it could be done consistent with their safety." Few Americans who visit England to examine those records learn how much they are indebted to that gentleman; because he had by his perseverance rendered himself unpopular among some influential officials, who considered his course an infringement upon their interest. Sir Harris Nicolas, as he was familiarly called, possessed those rare qualities of mind which seemed to endow him with an intuitive knowledge, to that wonderful extent to which few eminent men have attained through a long life. This naturally subjected him to the envy of some and the jealousy of others. And hence his enlightened views, put forth with regard to the public records, were combated from different quarters, and with some success. And yet the entering wedge, which he so powerfully drove into the heavy doors of the public archives, not only retains its place, but is pretty sure eventually to accomplish the great and beneficent object of forcing them entirely open. That Sir Harris had co-workers is true, but they can take care of themselves. These remarks are made, because it is thought that not many Americans appreciate the labors of that gentleman, as, most likely, they are unacquainted with them. The majority of his publications are now obtainable; but it is highly probable that when Antiquarian and Historical Societies are *advanced* enough to attempt to collect them, they will find them difficult to be had. The last place of residence of Sir Harris in London, was No. 55 Torrington Square, to which the devoted American antiquary will not fail to make a pilgrimage when he may visit the Metropolis of the British empire; or, rather, the Metropolis of the world.

The worlds suruaied bounds, braue Drake on thee did gaze,
Both North and Southerne Poles, haue seene thy manly face
If thanklesse men conceale thy prayse the starres woulde blaze
The Sunne his fellow trauellers worth will duely grace

Ro Vaughan sculp

It is not very surprising that the progress of collecting, arranging, and laying open to the public the muniments of the realm has been slow, if the magnitude of these muniments is but partially comprehended. Some idea may be formed on this head, by a comparison of our own records with those of England. This can be done only by a comparison of the length of time the two countries or governments have been in existence. A little reflection on this point may warrant the averment, that, if all the records of the United States were collected together, they would not occupy a space equal to that occupied by the British State Paper Office alone: to say nothing of the magnitude of those in the Tower of London, in the Rolls Chapel, the Chapter House, Remembrancer's Office, Treasuries of the King's Bench and Common Pleas Remembrance Office, Augmentation Office, British Museum, &c., &c.

New England, as is well known, was named by, or in the time of, Captain John Smith, who explored and surveyed its eastern coast. And Smith tells us the name was given because it had been already conferred on its western coast, by his great cotemporary, whom he characterizes as "the most memorable Sir Francis Drake." Such are Smith's own words.

Drake had discovered the opposite coast in the South Sea, (as the Pacific Ocean was then and long after called,) in the year 1579, took possession of it for the Crown of England, and named it New Albion—" in regard whereof," continues Smith, " this is styled New England"—Albion being an ancient name of England. Early grants of territory in America by James the First, extended from Sea to Sea; that is, from the Atlantic to the Pacific Oceans, and hence Captain Smith very naturally concluded that America, that is, the portion of it within the parallels of Drake's discovery, should bear the same name as that which he had given it. And thus originated the name New England; a name which, it is hoped, it will ever retain, as its appropriateness can never be questioned.

A list or catalogue of all the ships which brought emigrants to New England, from the time of its first discovery until emigration nearly ceased in the time of the Commonwealth of England, would be a document of great importance to every inquirer into the history of that country. And yet much greater would be the gratification were such a document accompanied by another, containing all the names of those emigrants But such lists cannot be hoped for, because they do not exist. What 1 have stated towards the close of this volume will probably satisfy inquir-. ers upon that subject.

However humble may have been the condition of those who fled to New England, in its primeval and savage state, to found a land for freedom of thought and action, their names will occupy a proud place in the History which is yet to be written. And ungrateful must be that descendant of those founders who will not, in some way, aid to rescue their names from oblivion, that they may be engraven upon the tablets of enduring annals.

The accompanying Map of New England is an exact copy of that published in 1625, in "Pvrchas his Pilgrimes." It shows the parts of America, as they were represented to our Fathers at the period of their emigration. It is not only interesting as showing what was then known of New England, but especially as it shows who were its then proprietors, those proprietors having their names inserted upon it. Captain Smith had published an earlier map, but it only faintly resembles this. The well known Hondius published a map of the world in 1589. On this the names New France and Florida cover all the country from Nova Scotia to Louisiana. But Smith's map was the first on which the name *New England* appeared. On a very early one, accompanying Father Pedro Apiano's Cosmographia, 1548, the countries now the United States, Canada, &c., are denominated "Baccalearum." This curious and singular map is pretty nearly copied by Sir Humfrey Gilbert, in his "Discourse of a Discoverie for a new Passage to Cataia," 4°, London, 1576. This last named work is of excessive rarity. The only copy which I have ever seen is in the British Museum. In Master Lewes Robert's "Mappe of Commerce," 1638, there is a handsome map of the world, on which New England is conspicuously laid down.

These are the Lines that shew thy Face: but those
That shew thy Grace and Glory brighter bee:
Thy Faire-Discoueries and Fowle-Overthrowes
Of Salvages, much Civillizd by thee
Best shew thy Spirit; and to it Glory Wyn;
So, thou art Brasse without, but Golde within.
If so, in Brasse, too soft smiths Acts to beare
I fix thy Fame, to make Brasse steele out weare.

Thine, as thou art Virtues.
  John Dauies Heref.

FOUNDERS OF NEW ENGLAND.

In a large volume bound in vellum, now in the Rolls Office, Chancery Lane, London, are records of a few of the early emigrants to New England. On the cover of the volume containing the earliest of such records yet discovered, is this inscription :—

"A Booke of Entrie for Paſsengers by yᵉ Comiſsion, and Souldiers according to the Statutiᵉ paſsing beyond the Seas, begun at Chriſtmas, 1631. and ending at Chriſtmas, 1632."

In it were originally about two quires of paper, all of which is filled with the records indicated on the cover. The front of the book appears to have been intended for the entry of names of soldiers. The other end for emigrants, travellers, traders, &c. The part containing these entries is entire. The volume is not paged,* but the dates follow in order, which is ample for reference. The first entry of names of persons for New England which I can find is on leaf 6th, and is as follows :

vij Marcij 1631.—The names of such Men as are to be transported to New England to be resident there vppon a plantacon, have tendred and taken the oath of allegeance according to the statute, vizt.

Thomas Thomas	Walter Harris	Thomas Haeward
Thomas Woodford	Joseph Mannering	Edmond Wynsloe †
John Smallie	John Levins	John Hart
John Whetston	Thomas Olliver	Willm̄ Norton
Wᵐ Hill	John Olliver	Robert Gamlin
Willm̄ Perkins		

* Nor are any of these volumes paged ; hence referring to pages would be referring to what does not exist.

† June 5th, 1632, the ship William and Francis arrived at Boston. Among the passengers was Mr. Edward Winslow. Prince, in *Hist. and Antiqs. Boston*, 140.

xij° Aprilis, 1632.—The names of such Men women and children wch are to passe to New England to be resident there vppon a Plantacon, have tendred and taken the oath of allegeance according to ye Statute

John Barcrofte	John Greene	Abigall Greene
Jane Barcrofte	Perseverance Greene	Sara Johnes *made servt.*
Hugh Moier	John Greene	Joseph Greene
Henrie Sherborn	Jacob Greene	

xxij° Junij 1632.—The names of such Men transported to New England to the Plantacon there p'r Cert. from Capten Mason have tendred and taken the oath of allegeance according to the Statute

William Wadsworth	Jonathan Wade	Thomas Carrington
John Tallcott	Robert Bartlett	William Goodwynn
Joseph Roberts	Jo: Browne	John White
John Coxsall	John Churchman	James Olmstedd
John Watson	Tobie Willet	William Lewes
Robert Shelley	William Curtis	Zeth Graunt
Willm Heath	Nic° Clark	Nathaniell Richardes
Richard Allis	Daniell Brewer*	Edward Ellmer
Thomas Vffett	Jo: Beniamin	Edward Holmar
Isack Murrill	Richard Beniamin	Jo: Totman
John Witchfield	William James	Charles Glower

[I have looked through the volume and can find no others for New England.]

The next volume, containing records of persons emigrating to New England, is also in the Rolls Office. It was formerly among the records and documents at Carlton Ride.† I should not say it was *found* there, for I am not aware that it was ever *lost,* but, like thousands of other papers and books of records, it was deposited there for safe keeping. But, during the two hundred and twenty-four years which have elapsed since the volume was made, it has, during some part of that period, not been very *safely* kept, for near a third of it has been damaged by laying long in water or a damp place; yet this damage does not extend but two or three inches from the foot of the first pages, and nearly the whole of it can be read.

The volume contains about three quires of foolscap paper, and is bound

---

* MS. perfectly plain.

† On the northerly side of St. James Park, now (1859) being demolished.

in vellum. The first entry in it is " xxix[th] Dec̄ebr: 1634," recording, that " *Wm Conasley*, aged 22 yeres," might " pass to Dort on his affairs."

The next entry (apparently made at the same time with the first) under the same date, is " *Samuell Sharpe* aged 55 years dwellen in London."

Several pages onward, date V° ffebr: [1634-5] is " *Samvel Sharp* 54 yeres old, dwelling in Layden."

About a third of the volume is taken up with recording the names of persons going to some part of the Low Countries,—Holland and Flanders, —some to reside and some to return. The last entry is of date 24th December, 1635.

The passengers for New England, Virginia, American islands, &c., are entered at the other end of the book. The first date there is " Vltiŏ Decembris, 1634," which is followed by a list of twenty-eight soldiers for " Guttorembeck." The list is prefaced thus : " Post festum Natalis Christi 1634. Vsqe ad festum Na: Christi 1635."

On the vellum wrapper or cover is this inscription :

" The Register of the names
of all y[e] Passinger[s] w[ch]
Passed from y[e] Port of
London for an whole
yeare ending at
Xmas 1635."

[The various companies " desirous " of leaving England are entered in the order of their application, or nearly so, and hence those for different parts are so mixed up that a close inspection of the whole is indispensable, in making out a list for any one destination. My search was only for those who went for New England, and I feel quite confident none have escaped me. And the readers of the Register may rest assured, that, though critical antiquaries may not fully agree as to what every name in these lists is, the following is a *full* and perfect copy of all the lists yet discovered.

For the examining reader's benefit, I have underscored the occupations, and some other words or sentences, believing that by that method some relief would be afforded to the eye. I have intended to keep to the old orthography and use of capital letters, presuming that the descendants of those emigrants will ever desire to know how the exact record stands, as it is an indication of the state of literature, at least among educated clerks, of that age.

The notes being all my own, throughout, this announcement is to avoid signing each of them, or otherwise advertising the reader. Quotation marks, too, are generally omitted, as the beginning and ending of the record is sufficiently apparent without them. Clerical abbreviations are printed to accommodate modern type.]

xj° Marcij 1634. Theise vnder written names are to be transported to New England, having brought Certificate from the Justices of the peace and Minister of the p'ish, the p'tie hath taken the oathe of Allegeance and Supremacie *de p'ochia St. Egiddij Cripplegate.**

Peter Howson xxxi yeres† and *his wife* Ellin Howson 39 yeres old.

Turris London Theise vnder written names are to be transported to New England having brought attestacon and Certificate from the Justices of peace and Minister of the p'ish according to the LLs of the Councells ord^r the p'tie hath taken the oaths of Allegeance and Supremacie.

Thomas Stares 31 yeres
Suzan Johnson 12 "

16 Marcij 1634. Theis vnder written names are to be transported to New England imbarqued in ye Christian de Lo. Jo^h White M^r bound thither, the men have taken ye oath [of] Allegeance & Supremacie. *Mildred Bredstret.*‡

ffrancis Stiles	35	Jo: Reeves	19
Tho: Bassett	37	Tho ffoulfoot	22
Tho: Stiles	20	James Busket	28
Tho: Barber	21	Tho Coop §	18
Jo: Dyer	28	Edward Preston	13
Jo: Harris	28	Jo: Cribb	30
James Horwood	30	George Chappell	20

* What I have underscored is in the margin, and *is* according to the MS.

† I have omitted to repeat the word "yeres" over the column of ages as entirely superfluous.

‡ In the margin of this list. St. Mildred's was destroyed in the great fire of 1666, and was rebuilt by Sr Chr. Wren.

§ Probably Cooper, but the MS. is as above, without abbreviation mark.

Robert Robinson	41	Henrie Stiles	40
Edward Patteson	33	Jane Morden	30
ffrancis Marshall	30	Joan Stiles	35
Ric^e Heylei*	22	Henry Stiles	3
Tho: Halford	20	Jo: Stiles	9 mo.
Tho: Haukseworth	23	Rachell Stiles	28
Jo: Stiles	35		

22° Marcij 1634. Theis vnder written names are to be imbarqued in ye Planter Nic° Trarice M^r bound for New England p'r Certificat from Stepney p'ish,† and Attestacon from S^r. Tho: Jay, Mr Simon Muskett Justices of the Peace. The men have taken the oathe of Supremacie and Allegeance.

Nicholas davies	40	James Lannin *A Glover*	26
Sara davies	48	Robert Stevens *A Sawyer*	22
Joseph davies	13	John More *A labourer*	24
Wm Locke	6	James Haieward	22
Jo: Maddox *A Sawyer*	43	Judith Phippin	16

4 Servants

Primo Aprill 1635. In the Hopewell of London m^r Wm Bundocke vrs‡ New England.

Jo^h Cooper   41 yeres
Edmond ffarrington   47   } of oney in Buckinghamsher theis have taken
Wm Parryer§   36   } the othe of Alleg. and Supremacie
Geo: Griggs   42 of Landen‖
Phillip Kyrtland 21 of Sherington } in Buckinghamsher.
nath: Kyrtland 19 of Sherington
Wibroe 42 yrs wife of Jo^h Cooper
Eliza: 49 yeis wife of Edmond ffarrington
Alyce 37 yeis wife of Wm Purryer
Tho: Griggs 15 yers
W^m: Griggs 14 "
Eliza: Griggs 10 "   } Children of Geo: Griggs aforsaid.
Mary Griggs 6 "
James Griggs 2 "
Alyce Griggs 32 wife of Geo: Griggs

---

* The MS. appears to me plain.
† Uniformly used for *parish*.
‡ Abbreviation of *versum* or *versus*. For, towards.
§ I need not apprise the reader that I aim to preserve the exact spelling of names.
‖ I do not find *Landen* in most minutely written topographical works, but I find *Laundon* in Buckinghamshire.

Mary Cooper 13 ⎫
Joh: Cooper 10 ⎬ Children of Joh: Cooper aforsaid
Tho Cooper 7 ⎬
Martha Cooper 5 ⎭
Phillip Phillip 15 yers sert to Joʰ: Cooper
Sarra ffarrington 14 ⎫
Mathew* ffarrington 12 ⎬ Children of Edm. ffarrington
Joʰ: ffarrington 11 ⎬
Eliza ffarrington 8 ⎭
Mary Purryer* 7 ⎫
Sarra Purryer 5 ⎬ Children of Wᵐ Purryer
Katheren Purryer 18 mo ⎭

2° Aprilis, 1635.—Theis vnder written names are to be transported to New England imbarqued in the Planter Nic°: Trarice Mr bourᵈ thither the p'ties have brought Certificate from the Minister of St Albonst in Hertfordshire, and Attestacōn from the Justices of peace according to the Lords Order.

Jo: Tuttell *A Mercer*	39	Mary Chittwood		24
Joan Tuttell	42	Tho: Olney *Shoemaker*		35
John Lawrence	17	Marie Olney		30
Wᵐ Lawrence	12	Tho Olney		3
Marie Lawrence	9	Etenetus Olney		
Abigall Tuttell	6	Geo: Giddins *Husbandman*		25
Symon Tuttell	4	Jane Giddins		20
Sara Tuttell	2	Tho: Savage *Taylor*		27
Jo: Tuttell	1	Richard Harvie *A Taylor*		22
Joan Antrobuss	65	ffrances Pebody *Husbandman*		21
Marie Wrast	24	Wᵐ Wilcockson *Lynen wever*		34
Tho: Greene	15	Margaret Wilcockson		24
Nathan Haford *seruant to* Jo: Tutell	16	Jo: Wilcockson		2
		Ann Harvie		22
Wᵐ Beardsley *A Mason*	30	Willm ffelloe *Shoemaker*		24
Marie Beadsley	26	ffrancis Baker *A Taylor*		24
Marie Beadsley	4	Tho: Carter	25	⎫ *Servants*
John Beadsley	2	Michell Willmson	30	⎬ to Geo:
Joseph Beadsley	6 mo:	Elizabeth Morrison	12	⎭ Giddins
Allen Perley *Husbandman*	27			*pred.*

3 Aprill 1635.
James weauer *Statinor* 23

---

* I need not apprise the reader that I aim to preserve the exact spelling of names.
† Now St. Albans.

Edmond weauer *Husbandman* 28 dwelling in Anckstrey* in Hereford-sher & his wife Margarett aged 30 yers

Theis vnder written names are to be transported to New England imbarqued in yᵉ Hopewell Mʳ Wᵐ Bundick. The p'ties have brought Certificates from the Minister & Justices of peace that they are no Subsedy † men they have taken the oath of alleg: and Supremacee.

Joʰ: Astwood *Husbandman*	26	Isuck Morris	9
Jo: Ruggells	10	Jo: Peat *Husbandman* of Duffill‡ p'ish in Derbieshere	38
Martha Carter	27		
Marie Elliott	13		
		Edward keele	14
p'r Cert: from Stanstede Abbey in com Hert.		Jo: Goadby	16
		Jo: Bill	13
Laurence Whittimor *Husbandman*	63	Tho: Greene	15
		Isacke Desbrough *Husbandman*, of Ell-Tisley in com Cambridge	18
Elizabeth Whittimor	57		
Elizabeth Turner	20		
Sara Elliott	6	Eliz: Elliott	30
Robert Day	30	Lyddia Elliott	4
Wᵐ Peacock	12	Phelip Elliot	2
Nazing in Essex.		Of St. Katherins	
Jo: Ruggells *Shoemaker*	44	Robert Titus *Husbandman*	35
Barbarie Ruggells *uxor*	30	Hanna Titus *vxor*	21
Jo: Ruggells	2	Jo: Titus	8
Elizabeth Elliot	8	Edmond Titus	·5
Giles Payson	26		

Geo: Woodward *fishmonger* 35 p'r Certi: from Sʳ Geo: Whitmor & Sʳ Nicᵒ Raynton two Justices of yᵉ Peace in London and from Jo: Thorp Minister of yᵉ p'ish of Sᵗ Buttolphs Billingsgate.

vjᵗʰ Aprilis 1635.

Theis p'ties heerevnder mencioned are to be transported to New England: imbarqued in the Planter Nicᵒ Trarice Mʳ bound thether: they

---

* Whether *Anckstrey* or *Auckstrey* is uncertain. The only name in Herefordshire bearing any affinity to this is *Akecitron* or *Arkston*, in Wobtree Hundred.

† Always so written in the original. And so "Allegeance." The serious difficulties between Charles I. and his Parliament about raising money, gave rise to this matter of subsidy. The reader of English history does not require even this intimation, perhaps.

‡ Probably *Duffield*, in Appletree Hundred.

have brought Certificates from the Justices of Peace and Ministers of ye p'ish that they are conformable to the orders of ye Church of England and are no Subsedy men: they haue taken the oath of Supremacie & Allegeance Die et An° pred.

Martin Saunders *A Currier*		40	ffrancis Newcom *Husb:*		30
Rachel Saunders *uxor*		40	Rachell Newcom	20	*wife &*
Lea Saunders	} *3 chil-*	10	Rachell Newcom	2½	*2 chil-*
Judith Saunders	*dren*	8	Jo: Newcom 9 monoths		*dren*
Martin Saunders		4	Ant° Stannion *A Glover*		24
Marie ffuller		17	Daniell Hanbury		29
Richard Smith	} *3 Ser-*	14	ffrancis Dexter		13
Rich Ridley	*vants*	16	Willm Dawes		15
			Marie Saunders		15

Theis p'ties imbarqued in the Eliz: Mr Wm Stagg bound for New England p'r Cert from the Justices and Ministers of ye p'ish.

Clement Bates *A Taylor*	40	Jo: Wynchester	19
Ann Bates	40	Jervice Gold *Servantes* *	30
James Bates	14 ⎫		
Clement Bates	12 ⎪		
Rachell Bates	8 ⎬ *5 children.*		
Joseph Bates	5 ⎪		
Ben: Bates	2 ⎭		

More for the Planter.

Richard Tuttell *Husbandman*	42	Tho: Tuttell	3 *mo.*
Ann Tuttell	41	Sycillie Clark	16
Anna Tuttell	12	Marie Bill	11
Jo: Tuttell	10	Phillipp Atwood	12
Rabecca Tuttell	6	Barthol: ffaldoe	16
Isbell Tuttell	70	ffrancis Bushnell *A Car-*	} 26
Marie Wolhouston	30	*penter*	
Willm Tuttell *Husbandman*	26	Marie Bushnell	26
Elizabeth Tuttell	23	Martha Bushnell	1
Jo: Tuttell	3½	Willm Lea	16
Elizabeth Swayne	20	Marie Smith	18
Margaret Leach	15	Hanna Smith	18
Ann Tuttell	2 *a qr.* [2¼]	Ann Wells	15

---

* The scribe made a brace against *Jo: Wynchester*, and began to write *servant* against that name, but stopped when he had written *se* and wrote *servants* against *Jervice Gold*.

In the Hopewell Willm Bundock Mr bound for New England, &c.

James Burgis	14	Marie Coke	14
Alexander Thwaits	20	Marie Peake	15
Jo: Abbott	16	Tho: Pell *A Taylor*	22
Jo: Bellowes	12	Jo: Bushnell *A Glazier*	21
Jo: Johnes	18	Christian Luddington,	18
Marie Abbott	16		

In the Rabecca of London Mr Hodges for New England.

Peter Vnderwood	*A Husbandman*	22
Isabell Craddock		30

vijth Aprilis 1635. This p'tie vnder mencioned is to be imbarqued in the Planter bound for New England p'r Cert: from Alderman ffenn of his conformitie he hath taken the oath of Allegeance & Supremacie.

Richard ffenn 27

8 Aprilis, 1635. Theis p'ties herevnder mencioned are to be transported to New England: imbarqued in the Elizabeth of London Wm Stagg M^r bound thither: they haue taken the oath of Allegeance and Supremacie p'r Cert: from the p'ish of St. Alphage Cripple gate the Minister there.

Wm Holdred *Tanner*	25	Daniell Brodley	20
Roger Preston *Tanner*	21	Isack Studman	30

That theis 3 p'ties p'rd. are no Subsedie men: wee whose names herevnto are written belonging to Blackwell Hall, do averr they are none.

Robte ffarronds
Thomas Smith

Theis p'ties herevnder written are to be transported in the Planter: p'rd. p'r Cert: from the minister of Kingston vpon Thames in the County of Surrey of their conformitie and y^t they are no Subsedy men.

Palmer Tingley* *A Miller*		21
Wm Butterick *An ostler*		20
Tho: Jernell *A Miller*		27

ixth Aprilis 1635. In the Elizabeth de London p'rd Mr Willm Stagg bound for New England: Theis vnder written names have brought Cert:

---

* I have no question as to this name, though the *T* is imperfectly made.

from yᵉ Minister of Hauckust* in Kent: and Attestation from two Justices of Peace being conformable to the Church of England and that they are no Subsedy men :

James Hosmer *A Clothier*	28	
Ann Hosmer *vxor*	27	
Marie Hosmer	2 } *two*	
Ann Hosmer	3 mo. } *children*	
Marie Dounard	24 } *two*	
Marie Martin	19 } *servants*	

John Ston	40
Edward Gold	28
Geo: Russell	19
Jo: Mussell	15

Nono die Aprilis 1635. In the Rabeca Mʳ Jo Hodges, bound for New England.

Jacob Welsh *husbandman*	32
Geo: Woodward	35

Theis vnder written names are to be transported to New England imbarqued in the Rabecca p'rd.

Elizabeth Winchell	52	Wᵐ Swayne	aged 16
Jo: Winchell	13	ffrancis Swayne	14

17th Aprill 1635. In the Eliza and Ane Mʳ Ro. Cowper† to New England.

Thomas Hedsall 47 yeres.

In the Encrease of London, Mʳ Robert Lea vrs New England.

Geo: Bacon‡	43 yers	Eliza: Ward *a maid servant*		38
Samuell	12 } *children of the*	Rebecca	18 }	
Joh:	8 } *said* Mason	Dorothy	11 } *Children of the*	
Susun	10 } [Bacon.]	Nathaniell	8 } *said* Tho:	
Tho: Jostlin§ *Husbandman*	43	Eliza	6 } Jostlin	
Rebecca *his wife*	43	Mary	1 }	

x° Aprilis, 1635. Theis vnder written names are to be transported in the Planter p'rd. Nic° Trarice Mʳ bound for New England p'r Cert. of the

---

* *Hawkherst* then, now Hawkhurst.

† *Cooper* elsewhere, but here it is *Cowper*.

‡ First written *Mason*, and afterwards erased and *Bacon* substituted; but the clerk omitted to do the same for the children.

§ See pedigree of Joselyne, in Register, vol. xiv. pp. 15, 16.

Minister of Sudburie in Suffolk and from the Maior of the Towne of his conformitie to the orders and discipline of the Church of England and that he is no Subsedy man; he hath taken the oath of Alleg: & Suprem:

Richard Haffell *Currier*	54		Alice Smith	40
Martha *vxor*	42		Elizabeth Coop	24
Marie Haffell	17	⎫	Jo: Smith	13
Sara Haffell	14	⎬ 5 *daugh-*	Job Hawkins	15
Martha Haffell	8	⎬ *ters*		
Rachell Haffell	6	⎪		
Ruth Haffell	3	⎭		

In the Planter p'rd: Theis vnder names are to be transported to New England:

Eglin Hanford	46	Rodolphus Elmes *	15
Margaret Hanford ⎱ 2 *dau-* ⎰	16	Tho: Stansley	16
Eliz: Hanford ⎰ *ghters* ⎱	14		

In the Elizabeth of London: Wᵐ Stagg Mʳ bound for New England.

Willm̄ Wild	30	Peter Thorne	20	Alice Wild	40

xjº die Aprilis, 1635. In the Eliz: pred. wᵐ Stagg Mʳ bound for New England: the p'ties vnder written have brought Certificate according to order.

Wᵐ Whitteredd, *carpenter*	36	Jo: Wild	17
Elizabeth *vxor*	30	Samuel Haieward	22
Tho: whittredd *sonn*	10	Jo: Duke	20
Jo: Cluffe	22		

In the Planter p'rd: Theis vnder written names are to be transported to New England p'r Certificate according to order.

Sara Pittnei	22	Margaret Pitnei	22
Sara Pittnei 7 ⎫ 2 Childn		Rachell Deane	31
Samvell Pittney 1½ ⎭			

---

* Settled in Scituate. See Deane's *History of Scituate*. His wife was Catharine, dau. of John Whitcomb, whom he married in 1644. Their ninth child, Rodolphus, b. 1668, settled in Middleborough, had wife Bethiah ——, and son Elkanah. This son had nine children.

xiij° Aprilis 1635. In the Elizabeth and Ann M⁵ Roger Coop bound for New England per Cert: from the Maior of Evesham in com͞ Worr and from the Minister of yᵉ p'ish of their Conformitie

Margerie Washborn	49
Jo: Washborne } sons {	14
Phillipp Washborne	11

In the Elizabeth de Lo.* Wͫ Stagg M⁵ prd. theis vnder written names brought Cert: from the Minister of St. Saviors Southwark of their conformitie

Tho: Millet	30	Joshua Wheat	17
Maria Millet *vxor*	29	Jo: Smith	12
Versula Greenoway	32	Ralph Chapman	20
Henrie Bull	19	Tho Millet	2

The vnder written named is to be imbarqued in yᵉ Increase Robert Lea M⁵ bound for New England p'r Cert: from Billerecay in Essex from the Minister of yᵉ p'ish that he is no Subsedy man.

Wͫ Rusco *husbandman*	41	Sara Rusco	9	
et vxor Rebecca	40	Marie Rusco	7	4 *children*
		Samvel Rusco	5	
		Wͫ Rusco	1	

In the Increase, prd. Theis vnder written names are to be transported to New England: p'r Cert: from All Sts Staynings,† Mark Lane of their Conformitie to the Church of England

Tho: Page *A Taylor*	29	Edward Spurkes	22	2 *ser-*
Elizabeth Page *vxor*	28	Kat: Taylor	24	*vants*
Tho: Page 2 } 2 *children*				
Katherin Page 1				

The Elizabeth and Ann Roger Coop M⁵. Theis p'ties herevnder expressed are to be imbarqued for New England having taken the oaths of

---

* *de Lo.* of London. London is often abbreviated so, and sometimes *Lon: Loñ.*, &c.

† *Allhallows* Stayning, probably. It escaped the great fire of 1666. In 1630 it was repaired and beautified, but not long after the fire, "it fell all down suddenly." *Strype's Stow's London.* It was anciently called the *stone* church; hence *stane* or *staying. Ibid.*

Allegeance and Supremacie and likewise brought Certificate both from the Ministers and Justices where their abidinges were latlie, of their conformitie to the discipline and orders of the Church of England and yt they are no Subsedy Men.

Robert Huwkynns *husb.*	25	Tho: Hubbard	10
Jo: Whitney	35	Tho: Eaton	1
Jo: Palmerley	20	Marie Hawkynns	24
Richard Martin	12	Ellen Whitney	30
Jo: Whitney	11	Abigall Eaton	35
Richard Whitney	9	Sara Cartrack	24
Nathaniell Whitney	8	Jane Damand	9
Tho: Whitney	6	Mary Eaton	4
Jonathan Whitney	1	Marie Broomer	10
Nic° Sension	13	Mildred Cartrack	2
Henry Jackson	29	Joseph Alsopp	14
Wm Hubbard	35		

In the Suzan and Ellin, Edward Payne Mr. for New England. Theis p'ties herevnder expressed have brought Certificate from the Minister and Justices of their Conformitie and that they are no Subsedy men.

John Procter *husb:*	40	Jo: Mansfield	34
Martha Procter	28	Clement Cole	30
John Procter	3	Jo: Jones	20
Marie Procter	1	Wm Burrow	19
Alice Street	28	Phillip Atwood	13
Walter Thornton *husb:*	36	Wm Snowe	18
Joanna Thornton	44	Edward Lumus	24
John North	20	Richard Saltonstall *husb:*	23
Mary Pynder	53	Merriall Saltonstall	22
ffrancis Pynder	20	Merriall Saltonstall	9 months
Marie Pynder	17	Tho: Wells	30
Joanna Pinder	14	Peter Coop	28
Anna Pynder	12	Wm Lambart	26
Katherin Pinder	10	Samvel Podd	25
Jo: Pynder	8	Jeremy Belcher	22
Richard Skofield	22	Marie Clifford	25
Edward Weeden	22	Jane Coe	30
George Wilby	16	Marie Riddlesden	17
Richard Hawkins	15	Jo: Pellam	20
Tho: Parker	30	Mathew Hitchcock	25
Symon Burd	20	Elizabeth Nicholls	25

Tomazin Carpenter	35	Grace Bewlie	30
Ann ffowle	25	Ann Wells	20
Edmond Gorden	18	Dyonis Tayler	48
Tho: Sydlie	22	Hanna Smith	30
Margaret Leach	22	Jo: Buckley	15
Marie Smith	21	Wᵐ Buttrick	18
Elizabeth Swayne	16		

15 May 1635. Penelopy Pellam 16 yers to passe to her brothers plantacō.

xiiij° Aprilis 1635. In the Increase of London Mʳ Robte Lea bounde for New England. Theis haue taken the oathes of Allegeance and Supremacye, and haue brought Certificat of their conformity wᶜʰ are this day filed.

Samuell Andrews	37	*Robert Cordell Gouldsmith in*
Robte Naney	22	*Limbert* street sent them a*
Robte Sankey	30	*Way.*
James Gibbins	21	

Also Jane the wife of the bouesaid Saml Andrewes   30
    Ellyn Lougie her Seruante aged   20
    Jane Andrewes her daughter aged   3
    Elizabeth Andrewes her daughter   2

        All for new land in the Increase aforesaid.

xvᵗʰ Aprill, 1635. In the Eliza. de Loñd. Wᵐ Stagg vrs New England. Theis p'tis haue taken oathe of Allegeance and of Supremacy before Sʳ Wᵐ Whitimort Sʳ Nich° Ranton.

Rich. Walker	24	Tho Lettyne	23
Joʰ Beamond	23	Joh: Johnson	23
Wᵐ Beamond	27	Willm̄ Walker	15

15 Aprill, 1635. In the Eliza: and Anne de Lond. Roger Cooper vrs New England.

Percy Kinge, 24 yers, a maid seruant to Mʳ Ro: Crowley.

---

  * So the MS.; no doubt *Lombard St.*, noted for jewellers.

  ✴ Easily taken for *Whitmore*, as the last *i* is not dotted; nor are half of that letter dotted in the whole MS.

In the Eliza: de Lond. Wm Stagg vers New England James Walker 15 yers and Sarra Walker 17 yers sernte to J^no Browne *Baker* and to on Wm Bracey *linnen drap* in Cheapside Lond. p'r cert. of their Conformitie.

viij° Aprilis 1635. Theis vnder written names are to be transported to New England imbarqued in the Increase de Lo. Robert Lea M^r. The p'te pred having brought Certificates from the minister Justices of ye Peace of his conformitie to the Church of England.

| Tho: Bloggett *Glover* | 30 | Daniell Blogget | 4 | } 2 chil- |
| Suzun Bloggett *vxor* | 37 | Samvell Blogget | 1½ | dren. |

In the Increase p'rd. The p'tie vnder written hath brought Certificate from the Minister of Wapping and from two Justices of peace of his Conformitie to ye Church of England to passe in ye said ship for New England.

| Tho: Chittingden *Lynnen wever* | } 51 | Isack Chittingden | 10 | } 2 *Children* |
| Rabecca Chittingden *vxor* | 40 | Hen: Chittingden | 6 | |

Theis vnder written names are to be transported to New England imbarqued in the Suzan and Ellin Edward Payne M^r. The p'ties have brought Certificates from ye Ministers and Justices of the peace of they are no Subsedy men: and are conformable to ye orders and discipline of the Church of England.

Ralph Hudson *A drap.*		42	Ben: Thomlins	18
Marie Hudson *vxor*		42	Edward Tomlins	30
Hanna Hudson	} 3 *Chil- dren.*	14	Barbara Fford	16
Eliz: Hudson		5	Joan Broomer	13
Jo: Hudson		12	Richard Brooke	24
Tho: Briggham		32	Tho: Brooke	18
Ben: Thwing	} *Servants.*	16	Symon Crosby *Husbandm:*	26
Ann Gilson *		34	Ann Crosby *vxor*	25
Judith Kirk		18	Tho: Crosby *child*	8 weeks
Jo: More		41	Rich: Rowton *Husbandm:*	36
Henry Knowles		25	Ann Rowton *vxor*	36
Geo: Richardson		30	Edmond Rowton *child*	6

* If this name is *Gilston* (and I know it is not) we should transcribe *Hudston, Atherston,* &c.

Percivall Greene *Husbandm*:	32	Ann Blason	27
Ellin Green *vxor*	32	Ben: Buckley	11
Jo: Trane } 2 *Servants* {	25	Daniell Buckley	9
Margaret Dix }	18	Jo: Corrington	33
Jo: Atherson	24	Mary Corrington	33

xv° Aprilis, 1635. Theis p'ties hereafter expressed are to be transported to New England in ye Increase Robert Lea M^r: having taken the oathes of Allegeance and Supremacie: As also being conformable to the Government and discipline of the Church of England whereof they brought testimony p'r Cert. from ye Justices and ministers where there abodes have latlie been. (viz.)

Samvell Morse *Husbm:*	50	Anna Payne	40
Elizabeth Morse *vxor*	48	Wm Payne	10
Joseph Morse	20	Anna Payne	5
Elizabeth Daniell	2	Jo: Payne	3
Philemon Dalton *A Lynnen weauer*	45	Daniell Payne	8 weeks
		James Bitton	27
Hanna Dalton *vxor*	35	Wm Potter	25
Samvel Dalton	5½	Elizabeth Wood	38
Wm White	14	Elizabeth Beardes	24
Marthaw Marvyn *Husbandm:*	35	Suzan Payne	11
Elizabeth Marvynn *vxor*	31	Aymes Gladwell	16
Elizabeth Marvinn	31	Phobe Perce	18
Mathew Marvynn	8	Henry Crosse *Carpenter*	20
Marie Marvynn	6	Tho: Kilborne *Husb:*	55
Sara Marvynn	3	ffrancis Kilborne *vxor*	50
Hanna Marvynn	½	Margaret Kilborne	23
Jo: Warner	20	Lyddia Kilborne	22
Isack More	13	Marie Kilborne	16
Samvell Ireland *Carpenter*	32	ffrancis Kilborne	12
Marie Ireland *vxor*	30	Jo: Kilborne	10
Martha Ireland	1½	James Roger	20
Wm Buck *Plowrite*	50	Richard Nunn	19
Roger Buck	18	Tho Barret	16
Jo: Davies *A Joyner*	29	Jo: Hackwell	18
Abram ffleming *Husband:*	40	Symon Ayres *Chirurgion*	48
Jo: ffokar *Husb:*	21	Dorothy Ayres	38
Tho: Parish *Clothier*	22	Marie Ayres	15
John Owdie	17	Tho: Ayres	13
Wm Houghton *Butcher*	22	Symon Ayres	11
Willm Payne *Husb:*	37	Rabecca Ayres	9

Jane Rawlin		30	Anna Ayres		5
Symon Stone *Husbm:*		50	Benjamin Ayres		3
Joan Stone *vxor*		38	Sara Ayres		3 *months*
ffrancis Stone		16	Steven Vpson *A Lawyer*		23
Ann Stone		11	Jo: Wyndell*		16
Symon Stone	*Children*	4	Isack Worden		18
Marie Stone		3	Nathaniell Wood	*Ser-*	12
Jo: Stone	5 *weeks*		Elizabeth Streaton	*vants.*	19
Christian Ayres		7	Marie Toller		16

17 Aprilis 1635. Theis p'ties herevnder expressed are to be transported to New England imbarqued in yᵉ Elizabeth Wᵐ Stagg Mʳ. Cert. from the Minister and Justices of the Peace of their Conformitie to the Church of England, they have taken the oaths of Allegeance and Supremacie.

James Bate *Husb:*	53	Mary Smith *filia*	15
Alice Bate	52	Peter Gardner	18
Lyddia Bate	20	Wᵐ Hubbard	35
Marie Bate	17	Rachell Bigg	6
Margaret Bate	12	Patience ffoster	40
James Bate	9	Hopestill ffoster	14
Edward Bullock *Husb:*	32	ffrancis White	24
Elizabeth Stedman	26	Joan Sellin	50
Nathaniell Stedman	5	Ann Sellin	7
Isack Stedman	1	Edward Loomis	27
Robert Thornton	11	Jo: Hubbard	10
Margaret Davies	32	Jo: Davies	9
Elizabeth Davies	1	Marie Davies	4
Dorothy Smith	45	Jo: Browne	40

The p'tie herevnder named with his wife and children is to be transported to New England imbarqued in the Elizabeth and Ann, Willm Cooper Mʳ. bound thither the p'tie hath brought testimonie from the minister of his conformitie to the orders and discipline of the Church of England and from the two Justices of peace yᵗ he hath taken the oaths of Allegeance and Supremacie.

Alexander Baker	28	Christian Baker	1
Elizabeth Baker *vxor*	23	Clement Chaplin	48
Elizaboth Baker	3	Wᵐ Swayne	50

---

* Possibly *Wendell*, but the MS. is perfectly plain *Wyndell*.

27 Aprilis, 1635. Theis vnder written names are to be transported to New England Roger Cooper M^r. bound thither in the Elizabeth and Ann. The p'ties have brought Certificates from the Minister at Westminster and the Justices of the Peace, of his Conformitie; the p'tie hath taken the oaths of Allegeance and Supremacie.

Richard Brocke *A Carpenter*	31	Daniell Preston	13
Edward Sall	24		

29 Aprilis, 1635. These vnder written names are to be transported to New England imbarqued in the Elizabeth and Ann, Roger Coop^r, M^r. The p'ties have brought Certificate from the Minister of the p'ish and Justice of Peace of their conformitie to the orders and discipline of the Church of England and y^t they are no Subsedy men.

Rich Goard*	17	Robert Lord	9
Tho: Lord *A Smith*	50	Aymie Lord	6
Dorothy Lord *vxor*	46	Dorothy Lord	4
James Cobbett	23	Wm Samond	19
Thomas Lord	16	Josias Cobbett	21
Ann Lord	14	Jo: Holloway	21
Wm Lord	12	Jane Bennet	16
John Lord	10	Wm Reeve	22
Joseph ffaber	26	Christopher Stanley *Taylor*	32
Tho: Ponnd†	21	Suzanna Stanley *vxor*	31

4° Maij, 1635. Theis vnder written names are to be transported to New England imbarqued in the Eliz: and Ann p'rd. The p'ties have brought Certificate from the Minister and Justices of the Peace of their conformitie and that they are no Subsedy Men.

Hen: Wilkinson *A Tallow Chandler*	25
Robert Haus *A Soape boyler*	19

Theis vnder written names are to be transported to New England: imbarqued in the Abigall, Richard Hackwell M^r. The p'ties have brought

---

* May as well be read Goare as Goard; for the terminal letter is *e* or *d*, and those letters are made exactly alike. The *d* is usually made a little taller than the *e*; but when used at the end of a word, and neither *d* nor *e* before occurring in the same word or name, it is not always possible to say which it is.

† The MS. is undoubtedly *Ponnt*; that being the name understood by the clerk. It is nothing uncommon to find *d* and *t* thus confounded.

Certificate from ye Minister and Justices of their conformitie to the orders and discipline of the Church of England.

Tho: Buttolph	32	Nathaniel Tylly	32
Ann Buttolph *vxor*	24	Peter Kettell	10
W^m ffuller	25	Tho: Steevens	12
Jo: ffuller	15	Eliz: Harding	12

6 Maij, 1635. Theis vnder written names are to be transported to New England, imbarqued in the Elizabeth and Ann, Roger Coop' M^r. The p'ties have brought Cert: from the Ministers where their abodes were and from the Justices of Peace of their conformitie to the orders and discipline of the Church of England and y^t they are no Subsedy men: they have taken the oaths of Allegeance and Supremacie.

Samvell Hull*	25	Rich Goard	17
Wm Swynden	20	Wm Adams	15
†Jo: Halsey‡	24	†Henry Curtis‡	27
Vyncent Potter	21		

viij° Maij, 1635. In the Elizabeth and Ann p'rd. Roger Coop' M^r. Theis vnder written names are to be transported to New England imbarqued in the said shipp: They brought Cert: of their Conformitie to the Church of England and y^t they are no Subsedy men.

John Wylie	25	George Orris	21
Jo: Thomson	22	Jo: Jackson	27
Edmond Weston	30	Elizabeth ffubin	16
Gamaliell Beomont	12	Grace Bulkley	33
Awdry Whitton	45		

Nono die Maij, 1635. Theis vnder written names are to be transported to New England, imbarqued in ye Suzan and Ellin, Edward Payne M^r. The p'ties haue brought Certificates from the minister of the p'ish of their conformitie to the Church of England, and that they are no Subsedy men: The p'ties haue taken the oaths of Allegeance and Supremacie.

Peter Bulkley	50	Richard Brooke	24
Tho: Brooke	20	Elizabeth Taylor	10
Precilla Jarman	10	Ann Lieford	13

---

* Certainly *Hull* in the original.   ‡ So marked in the original MS.†

In the Elizabeth and Ann p'rd. Roger Coop' M^r. bound for New England.

Robert Jeofferies	30	Suzan Browne	21
Marie Jeofferies *vxor*	27	Robert Carr *a Tayler*	21
Tho: Jefferies } *Children.*	7	Calebb Carr	11
Elizabeth Jefferies	6	Rich. White } *Carpenters*	30
Mary Jefferies	3	Tho: Dane	32
Hanna Day	20	Wm Hilliard	21

xj° Maij, 1635. Theis vnder written names are to be transported to New England imbarqued in the Eliz. and Ann p'rd. The p'ties have brought Certificate from the Minister and Justices of Peace of their conformitie to ye orders and discipline of the Church of England, and y^t they are no Subsedy men.

Willm Courser *A Shoemaker*	26
Geo: Wylde *A Husbandman*	37
Geo: Parker *A Carpenter*	23

xij° Maij, 1635. In the Elizabeth and Ann, Roger Cooper, M^r. bound to New England: Theis vnder written names are to be transported p'r Certificate from ye Minister of Bennandin* in Kent of their Conformitie to ye orders and discipline of ye Church of England.

John Borden	28	Jeremy Whitton	8
Joan Borden *vxor*	23	Mathew Borden	5
Nic° Morecock	14	Eliz: Borden	3
Bennet Morecock	16	Thomas Whitton	36
Marie Morecock	10	Samvell Baker	30

14 Maij, 1635. Theis vnder written are to be transported to New England, imbarqued in the Elizabeth and Ann, Roger Cooper Mr. The p'ties haue brought Certificatt from the Minister of the p'ish of their Conformitie to the orders and discipline of the Church of England.

Richard Sampson *A Tayler*	28	John Oldham	12
Tho: Alsopp	20	Tho: Oldham	10
Robt. Standy	22		

---

* Benenden, in the Lathe of Scray, Rolverden Hundred.

xv° Junij, 1635. Theis vnder written names are to be transported to New England: imbarqued in the Abigall de Lo: Mr H. Hackwell: The p'tie having brought Certificate from the minister of Thisselworth* of his conformitie to the orders and discipline of the Church of England. He hath taken the oaths of Allegiance and Supremacie.

Dennis Geere	30	Anne Pancrust	16
Elizabeth Geere *vxor*	22	Eliz: Tusolie	55
Elizabeth Geere } Children {	3	Constant Wood	12
Sara Geere	2		

19 Junij, 1635. Theis vnder written names are to be transported to New England imbarqued in ye Abigall: Hackwell Mr the p'ties having brought Certificate from the minister of the p'ish of the little Minories of his conformitie and opinion of the descepline of the Church of England.

Wm Tilly	28	Charles Jones	21
Robert Whiteman	20	Liddia Browne	16

Abord the James, Jo: May for N. England.

Tho: Ewer *Taylor*	40	Sara Beale	28
Sara Ewer	28	Elizabeth Newman	24
Elizabeth Ewer	4	Jo: Skudder	16
Tho: Ewer	1½		

xxth June, 1635. Theis vnder written names are to be imbarqued in the Abbigaill de Lo. Mr Hackwell, and boñd to New England, haue taken oathe of Allegance and Supremacie and Conformitie to ye Chh as p'adit from Two Justices of Peace and minister of St. Lawrence in Essex:

Henry Bullocke *husbandman*	40	Henry Bullocke } Children {	8
Susan Bullocke *his wife*	42	Mary Bullocke	6
		Tho: Bullocke	2

More xxth 1635. In the Desire de Lond. Pearce, and boñd for New

---

* *Thisselton* may be found mentioned in the Topographies of that time, but no *Thistleworth* or *Thesselworth*. *Thisselton* then, and *Thistleton* now, exist in Rutlandshire. But *Isleworth* in Middlesex was sometimes called *Thistleworth*.

Eng. p'r Cert. frō ij Justices of Peace and minister of All Saintes* lionian in Northapton.

Wm Hoeman *husbm:*	40	Hanna Hoeman		8
Winifred Hoeman *his wife*	35	Jeremy Hoeman		6
Alce Ashbey *maid Servant*	20	Mary Hoeman	5 *Children*	4
		Sarah Hoeman		2
		Abraham Hoeman		¼

---

xxth June, 1635. In the Abbigall de Lond. Hackwell bńd for New England p'r Cert. frō of his Conformitie from Justices of Peace and minister Eaton Bray† in Com̄. Bedford.

        Joh: Houghton   4 yers old

---

7 July, 1635. In the Defence de Loñd: Mr Edmond Bostocke vrs. New England p'r Cert. frō ij Justices of Peace and ministers frō Dunstable in Com̄ Bedfordshire:

Robert Longe *Inholder*	45	Anne		10
Eliza: Longe *his wife*	30	Mary		9
Luce Mercer *A seruant*	18	Rebecca	*Children*	8
Michell	20	Joh:		8
Sarra *Children*	18	Zachary		4
Robert	16	Joshua		¾
Eliza	12			

---

xxth June, 1635. In the Defence de Loñd. Mr Pearce vers New England p'r Cert. frō two Justices of Peace and minister of Towcester in Com̄ Northampton:

Joh: Gould *husbandman*   25   Grace Gould *his wife*   25

---

xxij June, 1635. In the Abbigall de Loñd. Hackwell vers New England p'r Cert. frō minister of Craiebroke in Kent.

---

* There were numerous churches in Northamptonshire called All Saints, but none at any place bearing a name approaching to *Lionian;* and I am not able to make the record other than I have transcribed it.

† Near, and to the west of Dunstable.

Edw: White *husbm:*	42		Joh: Allen *husbm:*	30
Martha White *his wife*	39		Anne Allen *his wife*	30
Martha White } *Children* {	10		Cert. Herrnhill* in Kent.	
Mary White	8			

In the Abigall, p'r Cert. from Justice peace and minister of Stepney :—

Geo: Hadborne *Glover*	43		Joseph Borebancke	24
Anne Hadborne *his wife*	46		Joane Jorden	16
Rebecca Hadborne } *Chil-* {	10		*Servants to Geo: Hadborne.*	
Anna Hadborne *dn:*	4			

22th. In the Desire de Lond Edw: Boswell vrs New England p'r Cert. from Sr Henry Mildmaye and minister of Baddow in Essex:

Joh: Browne *Taylor*	27	Anne Leake	19
Tho: Hart { *his ser-* {	24		
Mary Denny *vants*	24		

26 Junij, 1635. In the Abigall, Robert Hackwell Mr to New England p'r Cert. from Northton Tho: Martin, maior, and 2 Justices.

Jo: Harbert *shoemaker*	23	4th July Henry Somner	15
Richard Adams	29	Eliza: Somner	18
Suzan Adams	26		

17 Junij, 1635. Theis vnder written names are to be transported to New England, imbarqued in the Abigall, Robert Hackwell Mr p'r Cert. from the minister and Justices of Peace of their Conformitie, being no Subsedy men. They haue taken the oaths of Alleg: and Supremacy being all Husbandmen:

Ralph Wallis	40	Robert Mere	43
Ralph Roote	50	Samvell Mere	3
Jno ffreeman	35	Edmund Mañing	40
Walter Gutsall	34	Tho: Jones	40
Richard Graves	23	Geo: Drewrie	19

* Am not quite sure I have spelled this name as the Clerk intended to spell it, but I am *quite* sure that he meant *Hearnehill*, as it should have been written in those days. But in these *degenerate* days it is written *Hernhill*—thus farther departing from what it took its name originally.

Wᵐ Marshall	40	Elizabeth Ellis	16
Thomas Knore	33	Ellin Jones	36
John Holliock	28	Isacke Jones	8
George Wallis	15	Hester Jones	6
Rebecca Price	14	Tho: Jones	3
Marie ffreeman	50	Sara Jones	3 mo.
Elizabeth Mere	30	Cesara Covell	15
Jo: ffreeman	9	Joan Wall	19
Sycillie ffreeman	4	Wᵐ Payne	15
Jo: West	11	Noel† Knore	29
Mary Moninges	30	Sara Knore	7
Mary Monninges	9	Robt Driver	8
Anna Monnings	6	John Mere	3 mo.
Michelaliell* Moñinges	3		

In the Abigall p'red: p'r Cert: from the minister of their Conformitie and from the Justices that they are no Subsedy men:

Christopher ffoster	32	John Rookeman	45
ffrancis ffoster *vxor*	25	Elizabeth Rookman	31
Rebecca ffoster	5	Jo: Rookman	9
Nathaniell ffoster } childn: {	2	Hugh Burt	35
Jo: ffoster	1	Ann Burt	32
Edward Ireson	32	Wᵐ Bassett	9
Wᵐ Almond	34	Edward Burt	8
Mary Jones	30	Tho: ffreeman	24
Awdry Almond	32	Wᵐ Yates	14
Annis Almy	8	Elizabeth Ireson	27
Chri: Almie	3	Jo: ffox	35
John Strowde	15	Richard ffox	15
Edward Rainsford	26	Jo: Payne	14
Robt Sharp	20	Edmond ffreeman	45

Theis vnder written names are to be transported to New England imbarqued in the Blessing Jo: Lecester Mʳ. the p'ties having brought Cert. from the minister and Justices of their conformitie being no Subsedy men, tooke yᵉ oaths of Alleg: and Supremacie:

---

* Notwithstanding the strangeness of this name the MS. is perfectly plain. See another version of it in *Reg.* i, 132. See also *Reg.* vii, 273; viii, 75; x, 176.

† This christian name I read *Noel;* but it is impossible to be certain what it is. It may be the nick-name for Oliver. If so it is the earliest occurrence of its use known to me. The last letter was reformed, which is the cause of the indistinctness.

Willm Cope	26	Sara Robinson	1½
Richard Cope	24	Nico: Robertson	30
Thomas King	21	Jo: Mory	19
Jo: Stockbridge	27	Charles Stucbridge	1
Robert Saiewell	30	James Saiewell	1
Wm Brooke	20	Jo: Robinson	5
Gilbert Brooke	14	Ann Stockbridge	21
Nathaniell Byham	14	Suzan Saiewell	25
Jo: Wassell	10	Ann Vassall	42
W. Vassall	42	Suzan King	30
Rich: More	20	Judith Vassall	16
Robert Turner	24	Sara Tynkler	15
Eliza: Holly	30	ffra: Vassall	12
Ann Vassall	6	ThomazinMunson*	14
Margaret Vassall	2	Kat: Robinson	12
Mary Vassall	1	Mary Robinson	7
Elizabeth Robinson	32	Robt Onyon	26

29 Junij, 1635. Aboard the Abigall, Robt. Hackwell, Mr. for New England:

Joseph ffludd *A Baker*	45	Joseph ffludd	½
Jane ffludd *vxor*	35	Edward Martin	19
Elizabeth ffludd	9	Suzan Hathway	34
Obediah ffludd	4		

vltio Junii, 1635. Abourd the Abigall, Robert Hackwell Mr p'r Cert from the minister of Stepney p'ish of their conformitie: and that they are no Subsedy men.

Henry Collins *starch maker*	29	Joshua Griffith	}	{ 25	
Ann Collins *vxor*	30	Hugh Alley		27	
Henry Collins }	5	Mary Roote	} *Seruants* {	15	
Jo: Collins } *children* {	3	Jo Coke		27	
Margery }	2	Geo: Burdin	}	{ 24	

In the Abigall p'rd p'r Cert from the minister and Justices according to order.

Edward ffountaine	28	Thankes Sheppard *vxor*	23
Ralph Sheppard	29	Sara Shepperd *daughter*	2

* Plainly as I have transcribed it.

Primo die Julij, 1635. In the Abigall p'red.

Ann Gillam	28	John Cooke *servant*	17
Ben: Gillam *sonn*	1	Edward Belcher *servant*	8
Thomas Brune *husbandm:*	40	Ann Williams	10
Tho: Launder	22	Philip Drinker	39
William Potter *husb:*	27	Elizabeth Drinker *vxor*	32
ffrancis Potter *vxor*	26	Edward Drinker	13
Joseph Potter *weeks*	20	Jo: Drinker	8
Rich Carr	29	Margt: Tucker	23
Wm King	28	Ellner Hillman	33
George Rum*	25	Jo: Terry	32
Jo: Stantley	34	Jo: Emerson	20
James Dodd	16	Rich Woodman	9
Mathew Abdy	15	Elizab: ffreeman	12
Edward ffreeman *husb*	34	Alice ffreeman	17
Elizabeth ffreeman *vxor*	35	Hugh Burt	15
Edward ffreeman	15	Annis Alcoock	18
John ffreeman	8	Tho: Thomson	18
Jo: Jones	15		

Secundo die Julij. In the Abigall p'rd p'r Certificate from ye minister of Shoreditch p'ish and Stepney p'ish bound to New England.

John Deyking	28	Alice Steeuens	22
Jesper Arnold	40	Magaret Devocion	9
Alice Deyking	30	Ruth Bushell	23
Ann Arnold	39		

Theis vnder written names are to be transported to New England imbarqued in the Defence, Tho: Bostock Mr the p'tie hath brought testimony from the Justices of Peace and ministers in Cambridge of his conformitie to the orders and discipline of the Church of England: He hath taken ye oaths of Alleg: and Suprem̄:

Adam Mott *A Taylor*	39	Jo: Mott		14
Sarah Mott *vxor*	31	Adam Mott		12
Henry Steevens *mason*	24	Jonathan Mott	*children*	9
John Sheppard *Husbm:*	36	Elizabeth Mott		6
Margaret Sheppard	31	Mary Mott		4
Tho: Sheppard	*mo* 3			

---

* So the MS., and not *Ram*.

In the Defence p'rd Tho: Bostock M^r for New England p'r Cert: from the minister of ffenchurch of his conformitie, &c.

Tho: Boylson*   20

4th July, 1635. In the Abbigall de Lo: p'r Cert. from the minister and Justices of peace of St Ollives Southwark:

Ralph Mason *Joyner*	35	Richard Mason	} children {	5
Anne Mason *his wife*	35	Samuell Mason		3
		Susan Mason		1

In the Defence p'rd.

Elizabeth ffrench	30	ffrancis ffrench	10
Elizabeth ffrench	6	Jo: ffrench	mo 5
Marie ffrench	2½		

iiij July, 1635. In the Defence de Loñd. Mr Thomas Bostocke, vrs New England p'r Cert: from the minister and Justices of peace of his Conformitie to ye Govmt. of Church of Engl^d and no Subsedy man.

Roger Harlakendent   23 toke oathe of Allegance and Supremacie.
Eliza Harlakenden *his wife* 18 Mable Harlakenden *his sister* 21

Anne Wood	23	⎫	W^m ffrench	30
Samuell Shepherd	22	⎬ Servants to ye aforesaid Roger Harlakenden.	Eliza ffrench *his wife*	32
Joseph Cocke	27		Robert *a man servant*	
Geo: Cocke	25	⎭	Sarra Simes	30

---

* There will be found a pedigree of Boylston in the Hist. and Antiqs. of Boston, p. 726.

† In the *Visitation of Kent*, 1574, *Additional MSS.* (B. M.) *Vol.* 5532, *p.* 58 *b*, is the following pedigree:—

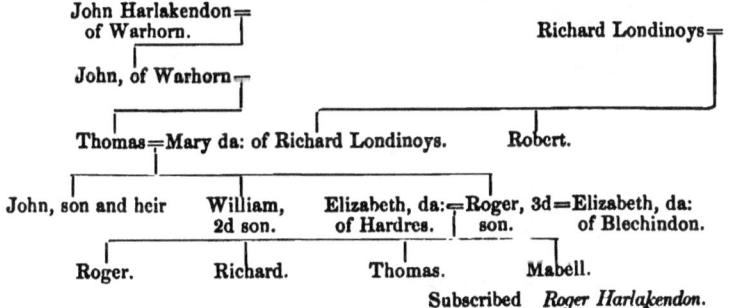

Subscribed   *Roger Harlakendon.*

6th July.   In the Defence de Loñd Mr Tho: Bostocke vrs. New England.
Joh: Jackson *wholesale man in Burchen Lane*   30
P'r Cert. from Sr Geo: Whitmore* and minister of ye p'ish.

---

x° July, 1635. In the Abigall, Richard Hackwell Mr p'r Cert: from the minister and Justice of Peace of his conformitie to the Church of England and that he is no Subsedy man.

John Wynthropp	27	Tho: Goad	15
Elizabeth Winthropp	19	Elizabeth Epps	13
Deane Winthropp	11	Mary Lyne	6

In the Defence p'rd p'r Cert from the Justices and minister of his conformitie in the Church of England:

James ffitch *A Taylor*	30	Abigall ffitch *vxor*	24

---

xj° Die July, 1635. Theis vnder written names are to be transported to New England imbarqued in the Defence of London, Edward Bostock Mr p'r certificate of his conformitie in Religion and that he is no Subsedy man.

Richard Perk *a miller*	33	Isabell Perk	7
Margery Perk	40	Elizabeth Perk	4
Henry Duhurst	35		

14 July, 1635. In the Defence de Loñd. Mr Edmond Bostocke vrs New England p'r Cert. from the minister:

Robert Hill *servant to Mr Craddocke*   20

---

xviij° July, 1635. Theis vnderwritten names to be transported to New England in the Pide Cowe p'r Cert: from the minister of his conformitie and from Sr Edward Spencer resident neere Branford that he is no Subsedy man: hath taken the oathes of Alleg: and Suprem.

William Harrison	55	Wm Baldin	9
Jo{h} Baldin	13		

Theis vnder written names are to be transported to N. England im-

---

* The same spelt *Whittimor* in a previous page.

barqued in the defence p'red. p'r Cert: from the ministers and Justices of their conformitie and y^t they are no Subsedy men :

Sara Jones	34		Mary Hubbard	20
Sara Jones	15		Robert Colburne	28
Jo: Jones	11		Edward Colborne	17
Ruth Jones	7		Dorothie Adams	24
Theophilus Jones	3		ffrancis Nutbrowne	16
Rabecca Jones	2		Wm Williamson	25
Eliz: Jones	½		Marie Willmson	23
Tho: Donn	25		Luce Mercer	19
Suzanna ffarebrother	25		Jo: ffitch	14
Eliza ffennick	25		Penelope Darno	29
Wm Sawkynn	25		Martha Banes	20
W. Hubbard *Hu,b:*	40		Jasper Gonn	29
Judith Hubbard	25		Ann Gonn	25
John Hubbard	15		ffebe Maulder	7
Wm Hubbard	13		Sym: Roger	20
Wm Read	48		Jo: Jenkynn	26
Mabell Read	30		Robert Keyne	40
George Read	6		Eliz. Steere	18
Ralph Read	5		Sarah Knight	50
Justice Read	*mo.* 18		Ann Keyne	38
Dorothie Knight	30		Ben: Keyne	16
Nathaniell Hubbard	6		Jo: Burtes	29
Richard Hubbard	4		Mary Bentley	20
Martha Hubbard	22			

13 July, 1635. Theis vnder written names are to be transported to N. England imbarqued in the James, Jn° May M^r for N: E: p'r Cert: from the minister of their conformity in Religion and that they are no Subsedy men.

Wm Ballard *husb:*	32		Rich. Terry	17
Elizabeth Ballard	26		Tho: Marshall	22
Hester Ballard	2		Wm Hooper	18
Jo: Ballard	1		Edmond Johnson	23
Alice Jones	26		Samvel Bennet	24
Eliza Goffe	26		Rich Palmer	29
Edmond Bridges*	23		Anto Bessy	26
Michell Milner	23		Edw: Gardner	25
Tho: Terry	28		Wm Colbron	16
Robert Terry	25		Henry Bull	25

* See Pedigree in New England Hist. and Gen. Register, viii, 252.

Salomon Martin	16	Nic. Goodhue *clothworker*	60
Wm Hill *wheele write*	70	Jane Goodhue	58
Nicº Buttry	33	John Johnson	26
Martha Buttry	28	Suzan Johnson	24
Grace Buttry	1	Eliza: Johnson	2
Jo: Hart *shoemaker*	40	Tho: Johnson *mo*	18
Mary Hart	31	Ralph ffarman *Barber*	32
Henry Tybbot *shoemaker*	39	Alice ffarman	28
Elizabeth Tybbott	39	Mary ffarman	7
Jeremy Tybbott	4	Tho ffarman	4
Samvell Tybbot	2	Ralph ffarman	2
Remembrance Tybbott	28		

Theis vnder written names are to be transported to N. England imbarqued in the Blessing, John Lester Mr. the p'ties have brought Cert: from the ministers and Justices of their conformitie in Religion and that they are no Subsedy men.

Jo: Jackson *Fisherman*	40	Mary Sprall	20
Margaret Jackson	36	Rich. Hallingworth	40
John Jackson	2	Suzan Hallingworth	30
Jo: Manifold	17	Christian Hunter	20
John Burules	26	Eliz: Hunter	18
Jo: ffitch	14	Tho: Hunter	14
Nicº Long	19	Wm Hunter	11
Christian Buck	26	Wm Hollingworth	7
Barnabie Davies	36	Rich Hallingworth	4
Suzan Daues	16	Suzan Hallingworth	2
Robert Lewes	28	Eliz: Hallingworth	3
Eliz: Lewes	22	Tho: Trentum	14
Edward Ingram	18	Tho: Bigges	13
Henry Beck	18	Jo: Brigges	20
Jo: Hathoway	18	Robt. Lewes*	28
Richard Sexton	14	Eliz: Lewes*	22
Mary Hubbard	24		

Theis vnder written names are to be transported to New England imbarqued in the Love, Joseph Young Mr.

Willm Cherrall *Baker*	26	Jo: Harman	12
Vrsula Cherrall	40	ffrancis Harman	43

* It is not probable that there were two Lewises named *Robert*, and two named *Eliz:* of ages 28 and 22 respectively, but such is the Record.

Sara Harman	10	Willm Browne *Fisherman*	26
Walter Parker	18	Mary Browne	26

23 July. Theis vnder written name is to be transportd to New England imbarqued in the Pide Cowe Mr Ashley the p'ty hath brought Certificate of his conformitie in Religion and Attestacon from the Justices that he is no Subsedy man:

Robert Bills *Husb:*   32

28 July, 1635. Theis p'sons herevnder expressed are to be transported to New England imbarqued in the Hopewell of London, Tho: Babb, M^r p'r Certificate from the minister of St Giles, Cripplegate, that they are conformable to the Church of England. The men have taken the oaths of Allegeance and Supremacie.

Thomas Tredwell *A Smith*	30	Tho: Blackly	20
Mary Tredwell	30	Tho: Tredwell	1

xjth Aug^d 1635. In the Batcheler de Lo: Mr Tho: Webb vers New England:

Lyon Gardner	36	Eliza: Coles* *their maid sert.*	23
Mary Gardner *his wife*	34	Wm Jope	40

Who are to passe to new England, haue brought Cert: of their Conformitie.

21 Aug^d 1635. In the Hopewell de Lo: Mr Babb vrs New England:

Henry Maudsley   24

Hath brought Cert. from the minister of his Conformitie hath taken the oathe of Allegeance.

xj° Sept: 1635. Theis vnder written names are to be transported to New England imbarqued in the Hopewell p'r Cert: from the ministers and Justices of their conformitie in Religion to o^r Church of England:

---

* The MS. cannot be mistaken.

42   THE FOUNDERS OF NEW ENGLAND.

and y^t they are no Subsedy men. They have taken ye oaths of Alleg: and Suprem:

Wm Wood *Husb:*	27	Isack Heath *Harms* maker*	50
Elizabeth Wood	24	Elizabeth Heath	40
Jo: Wood	46	Elizabeth Heath	5
Robert Chambers	13	Martha Heath	30
Tho Jn°son	25	Wm Lyon	14
Marie Hubbard	24	Grace Stokes	20
Jo: Kerbie	12	Katherin Hull	23
Jo: Thomas	14	Mary Clark	16
Isack Robinson	15	Jo: Marshall	14
Ann Williamson	18	Joan Grave	30
Jo: Weekes *Tanner*	26	Mary Grave	26
Marie Weekes	28	Joan Clevin	18
Anna Weekes	1	Edmond Chippfield	20
Suzan Withie	18	Marg With	62
Robert Baylie	23	Tho: Bull	25
Marie Withie	16	Joseph Miller	15
Samvel Younglove	30	Jo: Prier	15
Margaret Younglove	28	Richard Hutley	15
Samvel Younglove	1	Daniell Pryer	13
Andrew Hulls	29	Robert Edwardes	22
Anthony ffreeman	22	Robert Edye	25
Twiford West	19	Walter LLoyd	27
Roger Toothaker	23	Ellin Leaves	17
Margaret Toothaker	28	Alice Alboñ	25
Roger Toothaker	1	Barbary Rōfe	20
Robert Withie	20	Jo: fforten	14
Henrie Ticknall	15	Gabriell Reld†	18

xix Sept. 1635. Theis vnder written names are to be transported to New England imbarqued in the Truelove, Jo: Gibbs, M^r the men have taken the oathes of Alleg: and Suprem:

Thomas Burcherd *laboring man*	40	Elizabeth Burchard	13
		Marie Burchard	12
Mary Burchard	38	Sara Burchard	9

* Probably *arms maker*. The MS. is clear as I have copied it. It was not uncommon in those days for English people to add the *h* to such words in writing, as many do yet in talking, as *hit* for *it*, &c.

† Possibly Rele. If so the final *e* is rather tall.

Suzan Burchard	8	Obediah Hawes	mo 6
Jo: Burchard	7	Ralph Ellwood	28
Ann Burchard	mo 18	Geo: Tayler	31
Peter Place	20	Elizabeth Jenkins	27
Wm Beeresto- *Barstow*	23	Wm Preston	44
Geo: Beeresto - *Barstow*	21	Marie Preston	34
Edward Howe *husband m:*	60	Wm Bentley	47
Elizabeth Howe	50	Alice Bentley	15
Jeremie Howe	21	Margaret Killinghall	20
Sara Howe	12	Jo: Bentley	17
Ephraim Howe	9	Tho: Stockton	21
Isacke Howe	7	Geo: Morrey	23
Wm Howe	6	Richard Swayne	34
Jo: Sedgwick	24	Sarah Haile	11
Jeremy Blackwell	18	Samvel Grover	16
Lester Gunter	13	Eliz: Preston	11
Zacharia Whitman	40	Sara Preston	8
Sara Whitman	25	Marie Preston	6
Zacha: Whitman	2½	Jo: Preston	3
Rabecca ffenner	25	Wm Joes*	28
Tho: Tibbaldes	20	Robert Browne	24
Thomas Sterte	15	Tho: Blower	50
Jo: Streme	14	Edward Jeofferies	24
Ralph Tomkins *Husb:*	50	John Done	16
Kat: Tomkins *vxor*	58	Roger Broome	17
Elizabeth Tomkins	18	Dorothie Lowe	13
Marie Tomkins	14	Jo: Simpson	30
Samvel Tomkins	22	Tho: Brighton	31
Richard Hawes	29	Tho: Rumball	22
Ann Hawes	26	Edward Parrie	24
Anna Hawes	2½	Jane Walston	19

A small parchment volume (also in the Rolls Office) labelled on the cover " T G 27.979 ^A A D 1637—13 Car. I" is occupied with a record of persons " desirous to pass beyond seas." Its upper right hand corner has been destroyed, by which much of the record is gone. It consists of but sixteen written leaves, and much the greatest portion of them is taken up with the names of persons going into Holland. It was originally

---

* *Ioes* or *Joes*. I cannot torture it into *Ives*.

a beautiful document, all in a splendid hand. What is not destroyed of the title of the volume is

> "A Register of the - - - - - - - - - - - -
> of such persons a - - - - - - - - - - -
> and vpwards and haue - - - - - - - -
> to passe into forraigne partes - - - - -
> March 1637 to the 29th day of Septe -
> by vertu of a commission granted to
> Mr Thomas Mayhew gentleman."

The above extract will convey some notion of the extent of the injury which the book has received, from fire, acid or rats; probably acid.

The first entry is as follows:—

"March 28, 1637. The Examenation of Edmund Knappe: borne in great Killingham and there dewling, gent. aged 25 yeares, is desirous to passe into holland to sarue the States."

I will note only a few others not going to New England.

WRIGHT.—Isacke, to go to layden in holland, there to inhabit. He was of Norwich in Norfolk, was born there, but his age the acid has destroyed. He was a single man.

PAGE.—Anne, wife of Robart Page to go to holland to see her friends and to return.

ROBENSON.—John, of Rye in Suffolk, aged 22, tayler, to pass to Rotterdam to seek of his trade and to retorne.

BROWNE.—John, borne in Norwich, gent. aged 55 trauiles into the Lowe Cuntres as Post for Letters and other wyes and retornes as his byssenes p'mts.

About four pages are filled with similar entries, and then comes the following:—

"These people went to New England with William Andrews of Ipswich, Mr of the John and Dorethay of Ipswich, and with William Andrewes his Sone Mr of the Rose of Yarmouth.

"Aprill 8th 1637. The examinaction of John Baker borne in Norwich in Norffolcke, Grocar aged 39 yeres, and Elizabeth his wife aged 31 yeares with 3 Children, Elizabeth, John and Thomas, and 4 Saruants,

Marey Alxarson, aged 24 yeares, Anne Alxarson, aged 20 yeares, Bridgett Boulle aged 32 yeares and Samuell Arres aged 14 yeares ar all desiroues to goe for Charles Towne in New England ther to inhabitt and remaine.

" Aprill 8th 1637. The examinaction of Nicho: Busbie of Norwich in Norff. weauer, aged 50 yeares and Bridgett his wife aged 53 yeares with 4 children, Nicho: John: Abraham: and Sarath: are desirous to goe to boston in New England to inhabit.

" Aprill 8th 1637. The examinaction of Michill Metcalfe of Norwich, Dornix,* weauear, aged 45 yeares and Sarrath his wif, aged 39 yeares with 8 Children, Michill: Thomas: Marey: Sarrah: Elizabeth: Martha: Joane: and Rebeca: and his Saruant Thomas Comberbach, aged 16 yeares, are desirous to passe to boston in New England to inhabit.

" Aprill 8th 1637. The examinaction of John Pers of Norwich in Norff. weauear aged 49 yeares and Elizabeth his wife aged 36 yeares with 4 children, John: Barbre: Elizabeth and Judeth, and one seruant, John Gedney, aged 19 yeres, are desirous to passe to boston in New England to inhabit.

" April 8th 1637. The examinaction of William Ludken of Norwich in Norff. Locksmith, ther borne, aged 33 yeares, and Elizabeth his wife aged 34 yeares, with one child and one Seruant, Thomas Homes, are desirous to goe to Bostone in Newe England, there to inhabit and remaine."

The two next entries are partly gone.

" - - - - - of Norwich in Norff. cordwaynar, aged 28 years and - - - - - - with 4 children, Samuel, John, Elizabeth, and Debra, - - - - - - - aged 18 yeres, and Anne Williams, aged 15 yeres - - - - - England to Inhabitt.

" - ncis Lawes, born in Norwich in Norff. and thar liuing, weauer, aged - - - idda his wife aged 49 yeares with one child Marey and 2 seruants, Samuell Lincorne aged 18 yeares and Anne Smith, aged 19 yeares ar desirous to passe for New England to inhabitt.

" - - - - The examinaction of William Nickerson of Norwich in Norff. weauear aged 33 yeares and Anne his wife aged 28 yeares with 4

---

* *Dornick*, a kind of stuff used for curtains, carpets and hangings, so called from *Doornick*, or *Tournay*, a city in Flanders, where it was first made.—PHILLIPS AND KERSEY.—*Dornix.*—BAILEY.—*Dornock.*—OGILVIE.

children, Nicho, Robartt, Elizabeth and Anne; ar desirous to goe to Bostone in New England ther to Inhabitt.

Aprill the 8th 1637. The examinaction of Samuell Dix of Norwich in Norff. Joynar aged 43 yeares and Ioane his wife aged 38 yeares with 2 children Presella and Abegell, and 2 Saruantes William Storey and Daniell Linsey, the one aged 23 the other 18 yeares; ar all desirous to pass to Boston in New England there to Inhabitt.

Aprill the 11th 1637. The examinaction of Henry Skerry of Great Yarmouth in the County of Norff. Cordwaynar, aged 31 yeares, and Elizabeth his wife aged 25 yeares, with one child Henry, and one Aprentice, Edmund Towne aged 18 yeares, ar desirous to passe for New England to inhabitt.

Aprill the 11th 1637. The examinaction of John Moulton of Ormsby* in Norf. husbandman, aged 38 yeares and Anne his wife, aged 38 yeares, with 5 children, Henry, Merey, Anne, Jane and Bridgett, and 2 Saruants, Adam Gooddens, aged 20 yeres, and Allis Eden aged 18 yers; ar all desirous to passe to New England, there to inhabitt, and abide.

Aprill the 11th 1637. The examinacton of Marey Moulton of Ormsby in Norff. Wydow ageed 30 yeares and 2 Saruants; John Maston, aged 20 yeares and Merrean Moulton aged 23 yeares are desirous to go to New England to inhabitt and dwell.

Aprill the 11th 1637. The examinacton of Richard Caruear of Skratby† in the County of Norff. husbandman, ageed 60 yeares, and Grace his wife ageed 40 yeares, with 2 children, Elizabeth, ageed 18 yeares and Susanna aged 18 yeares, being twynes, mor 3 Saruants, Isacke Hartt, ageed 22 yeures, and Thomas Flege aged 21 yeares, and one Marable Vnderwood a mayd seruant, aged 20 yeares, goes all for New England to Inhabett and Remayne.

Aprill the 11th 1637. The examinaction of Ruth Moulton of Ormsby in Norff. Singlewoman aged 20 yeares, is desirous to passe for New England there to Inhabitt and dwell.

Aprill the 11th 1637. The examinaction of Robertt Page of Ormsby in Norff. husbandman, ageed 33 yeares and Lucea his wife aged 30 yeares, with 3 children, Frances, Margrett, and Susanna, and 2 Saruants, William

---

* In the vicinity of Norwich.
† Probably *Scrattley*, now *Scratley*, a part of Ormsby.

Moulton and Anne Wadd; the one aged 20 yeares the other 15 yeares, and are all desirous to passe for New England to inhabitt and Remaine.

Aprill the 11th 1637. The examinaction of Henrey Dowe of Ormsby in Norff. husbandman aged 29 yeares, and Joane his wife ageed 30 yeares, with 4 children and one Saruant Anne Maning, aged 17 yeares, are desirous to passe into New England to inhabitt.

Aprill the 11th 1637. The examinaction of Robertt - - - - - - Singleman, is desirous to passe - - - - - - - - - - - - -

Aprill the 11th 1637. The examinaction of Ellin Robenson of - - - desirous to passe into New England ther to - - - - - - - - - -

Aprill the 11th 1637. The examinaction of William Williames of great Yarmouth - - - - - - 40 yeares and Alles his wife aged 38 yeares with 2 children - - - - - - - - ar desirous to goe for New England to inhabitt.

Aprill the 11th 1637: The examinaction of Elizabeth Williames of Yarmouth in Norff. Single woman aged 31 yeares, is desirous to passe into New England ther to inhabitt and Remaine.

Aprill the 12th 1637. The examinaction of Kathren Rabey of Yarmouth, a Wattermans wydow, ageed 68 yeares, is desirous to passe into New England there to remain with her Sone.

Aprill the 12th 1637. The examinaction of Richard Leeds of great Yarmouth, marrinar, aged 32 yeares, and Joane his wife aged 23 yeares with one child are desirous to passe for New England and there to inhabitt and dwell.

Aprill the 12th 1637. The examinaction of Henry Smith of Newbucknam* husbandman, aged 30 yeares, and Elizabeth his wife ageed 34 yeares with 2 children, John and Sethe ar desirous to passe into New England to inhabitt.

Aprill 13th 1637. The examinaction of John Ropear of New Bucknam, Carpentar ageed 26 yeares and Alles his wife ageed 23 yeares, with 2 children, Alles and Elizabeth, are desirous to goe for New England, there to Remaine.

[Then William Lambard and Samuell Clarke wanted to go to Holland, and so a large number of others; the record of which occupies some eight pages. John Eyre of Norwich, grocar aged 40 wanted only to go

---

* This name will be found in late Topographical works under *Buckingham New*.

and see the country and if he liked, to stay; otherwise he would come back in 3 months. Simond Sewell of Carlton Rod in Norf. aged 30, wanted to go to Holland only to see his friends, and to return in 3 months. Thomas Browne of Carlton in Suff. aged 18, to go to Layden to see an " onckell" and to return in three months. Robertt Chapman of Norwich " weauear" aged 37, to go to Holland to see the country, &c. &c.]

These people went to New England with William Goose, M^r of the Marey Anne of Yarmouth.

[*Date gone.*] The examinaction of Thomas Paine* of Wrentom in Suffolcke weauear aeged 50 yeares, and Elizabeth his wife aeged 53 yeares with 6 children, Thomas, John, Marey, Elizabeth, Dorethey and Sarah are desirous to goe for Salem in New England to inhabitt.

May the 10th 1637. The examinaction of Margrett Neaue of great Yarmouth in Norff. wydow, aged 58 yeres, and Rachell Dixson—her grand child is desirous to passe into New England to inhabit.

May the 10th 1637. The examinaction of Beniemen Cooper of Bramton in Suffolck husbandman aeged 50 yeares, and Elizabeth his wife aeged 48 yeares with 5 children, Lawrence, Marey, Rebecca, Beniemen and Francies Fillingham his sone in Lawe aeged 32 yeares, allso his sister aged 48 yeares, and 2 seruants, John Kilin and ffeleaman Dickerson, are all desirous to goe for Salem in New England and there to inhabitt.

May the 10th 1637. The examinaction of Abraham Toppan of Yarmouth Cooper, aeged 31 yeares and Susanna his wife aeged 30 yeares with 2 children, Petter and Elizabeth, and one mayd saruant, Anne Goodin aged 18 yeares are desirous to passe to New England to inhabitt.

May the 10th 1637. The examinaction of William Thomas of Great Comberton in Worcestershire, husbandman, Singleman, aged 26 yeares is desirous to passe to Exerden in New England to inhabitt.

May the 10th 1637. The examinaction of John Thurston of Wrentom in Suff. Carpenter, aeged 30 yeares and Margrett his wife aeged 32 yeares, with 2 children, Thomas, and John, ar desirous to passe to New England to inhabett.

May the 10th 1637. The examinaction of Luce Poyett of Norwich, spinster, aeged 23 yeares is desirous to pass into new England and there to Remaine.

---

* See N. Eng. Hist. and Gen. Reg., vol. v, p. 331.

May the 10th 1637. The examinaction of John Borowe of Yarmouth, Cooper, ageed 28 yeares, and Anne his wife ageed 40 yeures is desirous to passe to Salam in new England, there to inhabitt.

May the 11th 1637. The examinaction of William Gault of Yarmouth, Cordwaynar, Singleman, ageed 29 yeares, is desirous to passe to new England and there to remayne.

May the 11th 1637. The examinaction of Joane Ames of Yarmouth, Wydow, ageed 50 years, with 3 children, Ruth, ageed 18 yeares, William and John; are desirous to passe for new England and there to inhabitt and Remaine.

May the 11th 1637. The examinaction of Augusten C · · · · · Alles his wife ageed 40 yeares · · · · · · · · · · · · desirous to goe to Salam in New E · · · · · · · · · · ·

May the 11th 1637. The examinaction of John Darrell of · · · · passe into Salam in New England and there · · · · · · · ·

May the 11th 1637. The examinaction of John Gedney of Norwich in Norff. · · · · · · · · · · to passe for New England with his wife Sarah ageed 25 yeares · · · · · · · Lediah, Hanah and John; mor 2 Seruants; William Walker aged · · · · · Burges aged 26 yeares are desirous to passe for Salam.

May the 11th 1637. The examinaction of Samuell Aiers* of Norwch an apintes, aged 15 yeares ar desirous to passe into New England to his Mr John Baker, as he had apointed him.

The examinaction of John Yonge of St Margretts, Suff. minister, aged 35 yeares and Joan his wife ageed 34 yeares with 6 children, John, Tho: Anne, Rachell, Marey, and Josueph, ar desirous to passe for Salam in New England to inhabitt.

[*Against the above entry, in the place of the date is written:*—] This man was forbyden passage by the Commisionrs and went not from Yarmouth.

May the 12th 1637. The examinaction of Samuell Grenfild of Norwich, weauear, ageed 27 yeares and Barbrey his wife ageed 35 yeares with two children; Marey, and Barbrey, and John Teed, his seruant, aged 19 yeares, ar all desirous to passe into New England to inhabitt.

May the 12th 1637. The examinaction of Thomas Joanes of Elzing in

---

* Nearly obliterated in the original, but I feel quite sure it is *Aiers.*

Norff. Buchar, Singleman, ageed 25 yeres, is desirous to passe into New England and there to Remaine.

May the 13th 1637. The examinaction of Thomas Olliuer of Norwich Calinder, aged 36 yeares and Marey his wife ageed 34 yeares, with 2 children, Tho: and John, and 2 seruants, Thomas Doged, aged 30 yeares, and Marey Sape, ageed 12 yeares, ar desirous to passe for New England to inhabett.

May the 15th 1637. The examinaction of William Cockram, of Southould in Suff. marinar, ageed 28 yeers, and Christen his wife, ageed 26 yeares, with 2 children and 2 Seruantes desirous to passe to new england to inhabitt.

[Then succeeds a list for Holland, &c. Thomas Walter of Norwich, Cordwaynar, aged 30, to go to Rotterdam to see some friends, to be gone 3 months. Anne Thompson and her dau. Bridgett, to go to Holland to see friends, for 2 months. Anne Thompson was the wife of John, and of the age of 60. They were of Yarmouth. Geo: Bartton of Wollerbe in Lincolnshire was allowed 2 months, to go to Holland " to parfett some acountes." His age 41. "Joseph Hayward of Norwich, dorinx weauear, aged 29," his wf. Sussanna, 26, and servant, Ester Brown, 21, to go to Rotterdam to inhabet. Elizabeth Fowlsom, wf. of Tho. Fowlsome, of Norwich, aged 27, to go to Newport in Flanders, and Bombake" to " seeck menes whych is left[?] her by a kinsman. Henry Ward of Worttwell in Norff. aged 19, to goe ouer Sarue the Stattes." Christopher Hatton of Norwich a pot sellers of earthen Vessells borne in Bradish in Norff. ageed about 36 yeares" to pass to Holland to buy commodities, and to return in a month. 17 May, 1623. John Checklie, aged xx yeeres, intending to passe over to Rotterdam to serve as a souldier hath tendred and taken the oath of allegeance, &c. &c. At the end of the entries is the Signature " Henry Hill Deputy for Mr Thomas Mayhew, Gentleman."

The following Lists of New England Emigrants are from Her Majesty's State Paper Office. They cannot be referred to by volumes at present, as the papers, among which they are, are undergoing a re-arrangement; a condition which usually precludes examinations. But through the kindness of MR. SAINSBURY, under whose supervision they are being arranged and calendered, I have been indulged with the privilege of examinations, and allowed to make copies.]

IPSWICH.—A note of the names and ages of all the Passengers which tooke shipping in the Elizabeth of Ipswich Mr Williā Andrews bound for new Eng Land the last of Aprill, 1634.

John Sherman aged yeeres	20	Robert Sherin	32
Joseph Mosse	24	Humphry Bradstreet	40
Richard Woodward	45	Bridgett [Bradstreet] *his wife*	30
Rose [Woodward]* *his wife*	50	Henery Glouer	24
Edmond Lewis	33	William Blomfield	30
Mary [Lewis] *his wife*	32	Sarah [Blomfield] *his wife*	25
John Spring	45	Robert Day	30
Elinor [Spring] *his wife*	46	Mary [Day] *his wife*	28
Thurston Raynor	40	Sarah Reynolds	20
Elizabeth [Raynor] *his wife*	36	Robert Goodall	30
Thomas Skott	40	Katherin [Goodall] *his wife*	28
Elizabeth [Skott] *his wife*	40	Samuell Smithe	32
Henery Kemball	44	Elizabeth [Smithe] *his wife*	32
Susan [Kemball] *his wife*	35	Thomas Hastings	29
Richard Kemball	39	Susan [Hastings] *his wife*	34
Vrsula [Kemball] *his wife*		Susan Munson	25
Isaacke Mixer	31	Martin Vnderwood	38
Sarah [Mixer] *his wife*	33	Martha [Vnderwood] *his wife*	31
Martha Scott	60	Henery Gouldson	43
George Munninge	37	Anne [Gouldson] *his wife*	45
Elizabeth [Munninge] *his wife* •	41	Anne Gouldston	18
		William Cutting	26
John Bernard	30	John Palmer	24
Phebe [Bernard] *his wife*	27	Danyell Pierce	23
Thomas Kilborne	24	John Clearke	22
Elizabeth [Kilborne] *his wife*	20	John ffirmin	46
John Crosse	50	Rebecca Isaacke	36
Annè [Crosse] *his wife*	38	Anne Dorifall	24

These p'sons aboue named tooke the Oath of Allegeance and Supremacy, at his Ma'ts Custome house in Ipswich before vs his Ma'ties Officers according to the order of the Lords and others of his Ma'ts most Honoble Priuy Councell: This xijth of Nouember 1634.

Ipswich Custome House   Tho Clere, Sec
  Phil. Browne   Edw: Man
  p'r Custor.   Compt.

---

* For the sake of uniformity I have added the surnames of wives. I may have omitted the brackets in some cases. If so, it can lead to no error.

IPSWICH.—A Note of all the names and ages of all those which did not take the Oath of Allegiance or Supremacy being vnder age shipped in o' Port. In the Elizabeth of Ipswich M' Williā Andrewes bound for new England the last of Aprill 1634.

Ed: Lewis	John Lewis	aged 3 yeeres
	Thomas Lewis	3 quarters
Rich: Woodward	George Woodward	13
	John Woodward	13
John Spring	Mary Spring	11
	Henry Spring	6
	John Spring	4
	William Spring	3 quarters
Thurston Raynor	Thurston Rayner	13
	Joseph Raynor	11
	Elizabeth Raynor	9
	Sarah Raynor	7
	Lidia Raynor	1
	Edward Raynor	10
	Elizabeth Kemball	13
Tho: Scott	Elizabeth Scott	9
	Abigail Scott	7
	Thomas Scott	6
	Isaac Mixer	4
Hen: Kemball	Elizabeth Kemball	4
	Susan Kemball	1 and halfe
	Richard Cutting	11
Rich: Kemball	Henry Kemball	15
	Richard Kemball	11
	Mary Kemball	9
	Martha Kemball	5
	John Kemball	3
	Thomas Kemball	1
	John Lauericke	15
Geo: Munnings	Eliz: Munnings	12
	Abigail Munnings	7
Jno: Bernard	John Bernard	2
	Samuell Bernard	1
	Tho: King	15
Humph: Bradstreet	Anna Bradstreet	9
	John Bradstreet	3
	Martha Bradstreet	2
	Mary Bradstreet	1
Willi: Blomfield	Sarah Bloomfield	1

THE FOUNDERS OF NEW ENGLAND.

Sam: Smith	Samuell Smith	9
	Mary Smith	4
	Eliz: Smith	7
	Phillip Smith	1
Robt: Goodale	Mary Goodale	4
	Abraham Goodale	2
	Isaacke Goodale	half a yeere
Hen: Gouldson	Mary Gouldson	15

Ipswich Customehouse this xijth of Nouember 1634.

Phil: Browne   Tho: Clere, Sec.
p'r Custor.   Edw: Man
                   Compt.

IPSWICH.—A Note of the names and ages of all the Passengers which tooke shipping In the ffrancis of Ipswich, Mr John Cutting bound for new England the last of Aprill, 1634.

John Beetes aged yeeres	40	Robert Pease	27
William Haulton	23	Hugh Mason	28
Nicholas Jennings	22	Hester [Mason] *his wife*	22
William Westwoode	28	Rowland Stebing	40
Bridgett [Westwoode] *his wife*	32	Sarah [Stebing] *his wife*	43
Cleare Drap	30	Thomas Sherwood	48
Robert Rose	40	Alice [Sherwood] *his wife*	47
Margery [Rose] *his wife*	40	Thomas King	19
John Bernard	36	John Mapes	21
Mary [Bernard] *his wife*	38	Mary Blosse	40
William ffrebourne	40	Robert Cooe	38
Mary [ffrebourne] *his wife*	33	Anna [Cooe] *his wife*	43
Anthony White	27	Mary Onge	27
Edward Bugbye	40	Thomas Boyden	21
Rebecca [Bugbye] *his wife*	32	Richard Wattlin	28
Abraham Newell	50	John Lyuermore	28
ffrancis [Newell] *his wife*	40	Richard Pepy	27
Just Houlding	23	Mary [Pepy]	30
John Pease	27	Richard Houlding	25
Robert Winge	60	Judeth Garnett	26
Judith [Winge] *his wife*	43	Eliz: Hamond	47
John Greene	27	Thurston Clearke	44

These p'sons aboue named tooke the Oath of Allegance and Supremacy at his Ma'ties Custome house in Ips^{wch} before vs his Ma'ties Officers according to the order of the Lords and others of his Ma'ties most hono^{ble} Priuy Councell the xij^{th} of Nouember 1634.

 Ipswich Custome house   Tho: Clere, Sec.
  Phil: Browne   Edw: Mann Compt.
   p'r Custr.

IPSWICH.—A Note of all the names and ages of all those which Did not take the Oath of Allegiance or Supremacy being vnder age shipped in our Port In the ffrancis of Ipswich Mr John Cutting: bound for new England the last of Aprill, 1634.

Will: Westwood	John Lea	13
	Grace Newell	13
	John Rose	15
	Robert Rose	15
	Eliz: Rose	13
	Mary Rose	11
Robt: Rose	Samuell Rose	9
	Sarah Rose	7
	Danyell Rose	3
	Darcas Rose	2
	Mary ffreebourne	7
Will: ffreebourn	Sarah ffreebourne	2
	John Aldburgh	14
Jn°: Bernard	ffayth Newell	14
	Henry Haward	7
	Abraham Newell	8
Abraha: Newell	John Newell	5
	Isaacke Newell	2
Edward Bugby	Sarah Bugbye	4
	ffayth Clearke	15
John Pease	Robert Pease	3
	Darcas Greene	15
	Thomas Stebing	14
	Sarah Stebing	11
Rowland Stebing	Eliz: Stebing	6
	John Stebing	8
	Mary Winche	15
Mary Blosse	Richard Blosse	11
	Anna Sherwood	14
Tho: Sherwood	Rose Sherwood	11
	Thomas Sherwood	10
	Rebecca Sherwood	9

Robt: Cooe	{ John Cooe	8
	{ Robert Cooe	7
	{ Beniamin Cooe	5
Rich: Pepper	{ Mary Pepy	3 and half
	{ Stephen Beckett	11
Eliz: Hamond	{ Eliz: Hamond	15
	{ Sarah Hamond	10
	{ John Hamond	7

Ipswich Customehouse this xijth of Nouember 1634.

    Phil: Browne   Edw Mann* Compt.

      p'r Custr.

[The preceding lists are accompanied by a paper bearing the following record :—]

To the right houno^{ble} the Lords and others of his ma^{ties} moste honno^{ble} privie Councell.

The humble peticon and Certificates of John Cuttinge M^r of the shipp called the ffrancis, and William Andrewes Ma^r of the Elizabeth, both of Ipsw^{ch}.

Right houno^{ble} accordinge to yor Lo^{pps} order wee heerewth presente vnto yor Lo^{pps} the names of all the Passengers that wente for newe England in the said shipps the Tenth daye of Aprill laste paste.

Humblie intreatinge yor Lo^{pps} (they havinge p'formed yor honno^{rs} order) that the bondes in that behalfe given may bee delivered back to yor peticon^{rs}.

And they as in dutie bound will daylie praye for yor houno^{rs} healthes and happynes.

SOUTH^{ON}.—A List of names of suche Passeng^{rs} as shipt themselues at the towne of Hampton, in the James of London of iij^c tonnes William Coop^r M^r v^{rs} New-England, in and abouto the v^t of Aprill, 1635.

Augustine Clem^t, sometime of Readinge† *Paynter*	Thomas Browne, of Malford,‡ *weav^r*
Thomas Whealer *his servant*	Hercules Woodman, of the same, *mercer*

---

* An evidence that the same *Mann* did not always spell his own name alike.

† In Berkshire.   ‡ Perhaps *Milford* in Hants.

John Euered alias ⎫
Stephen Euered ⎬ Webb* of
Gyles Butler   Marlbo-
George Coussens   rought†
Thomas Colman   laborers
Thomas Goddard   or hus-
John Pithouse   bandmen

Anthony Morse ⎱ of Marlborough
William Morse ⎰ shoomakers.
John Hide, Tayler, ⎫
John Parker, Car- ⎪
  penter   ⎪
Richard Walker,   ⎬ late of
  shomaker   ⎪ Marl-
Maudit Ingles,‡   ⎪ brough
  ffuller   ⎪
Thomas Davyes,   ⎭
  Sawyer
Thomas Carpenter, of Ams-
  bury,§ Carpenter
William Paddey, ⎫
  skinnr [Cutler ⎬ late of
Edmund Hawes,   ⎭ London
Edmund Batter, maulter ⎫
John Smale, his servant ⎪
Michael Shafflin, Tayler⎪
Josuah Verren, Repr.   ⎬ late
Thomas Antram, weavr   ⎪ of
Thomas Browne, his   ⎪ New-
  servant   ⎪ Eng-
George Smythe, Tayler   ⎪ land.
Phillip Varren, Roopr   ⎪
John Greene, surgeon   ⎭

Zacheus Courtis, of Downton,‖
  laborer
Henry Rose, of Platford,**
  laborer
Nicholas Batt, of ye Devyes,
  lennen weavr
Thomas Scoates, of Sarñ,††
  laborer
John Pike,   ⎱ of Lang-
John Musselwhite, ⎰ ford,‡‡
                    laborers
Sampson Salter, of Caver-
  sham,§§ fisherman
Henry Kinge of Brencsley laborer
William Andrews of Hamps-
  worth, Carpenter
John Knight   ⎱ of Romsey,
Richard Knight ⎰ taylers
Thomas Smithe of the same,
  weaver
Nicholas Holte, thereof, tanner
Robert ffield of yealing, laborer
Anthony Thetcher of Sarm,
  tayler and
Peter Higdon his servant
James Browne   ⎱ youths of
Lawrence Seagr ⎰ Hampton
                 of about 17
                 yeares old.
Henry Leüage   ⎱ of Sarñ
William Parsons ⎰ Taylers
John Emery   ⎱ of Romsey,
Anthony Emery ⎰ Carpenters.
William Kemp servant

---

* John Evered alias Webb settled at Chelmsford, Mass., and died 1668. J. W. D.

† In Wiltshire.

‡ A name which has been subjected to much torture. Plain MAUDIT *Ingles* on this (original) record. On our (Boston) records, 2 April, 1638, *Maudit* Ings appears. No doubt the same. See *History and Antiquities of Boston*, 241, and elsewhere.

§ *Amesbury*, in Wilts.

‖ Several places bear this name, but *this* probably is in Wilts.

** Or *Plaitford*, in Wilts.   †† *Sarum*, Salisbury, in Wilts.

‡‡ Some twelve places bear this name in different counties. *Longford-steple* is in Wilts.   §§ Probably the same place called *Goñsham* in another list. In Oxfordshire.

The totall number of these men, youthes, and boyes are liij p'sons, besids the wives and Children of Dyvers of these.

Tho: Wurfris Coll^r ibm.   N. Dingley Compt^r
John Knapp Searcher

[*On a separate sheet accompanying the above:—*]
Right ho^{rble}

After the p'formance of our most humble Duties, may it please y^r Lo^{ps} to receaue hereinclosed a list of the names of suche passeng^{rs} as tooke shippinge at this porte for New-England, and that onely in Aprill last in the good ship Called the James of London whereof William Coop^r went M^r. And thus in Due obedience and observance of yor hon^{rs} lre Dated the last of Decemb^r past. Thus wee humbly take leave. Southampton the xijth Day of June, 1635.

Yo^r Lo^{ps} most humble serv^{ts}
Tho: Wurfris, Coll^r
N. Dingley, Compt^r
John Knapp, Searcher

[*Direction.*] To the right ho^{rble} the lords of his ma^{ts} most honorable privie Counsell, this at Whitehall. London.

[The following list of Emigrants was printed in the New England Hist. and Gen. Register, vol. ii, 108, &c., but from a copy so erroneous, it was determined to reprint it in this place.]

The List of the Names of the Passeng^{rs} Intended for New England in the good shipp the Confidence of London of C C. tonnes, John Jobson, Mr And thus by vertue of the Lord Treas^{rs} warr^t of the xjth of Aprill, 1638.

Southampton, 24° Aprill, 1638.

Ages.

Walter Hayne of Sutton Man-difeild* in the County of Wilts *Lennen weauer*	55	John Blanford } *their*	27
		John Riddet }	26
		Rich Bidlcombe } *seruants*	16
Eliz: Hayne *his wife*			
Thomas Hayne } *their sonnes*		Peter Noyce of Penton in the County of Southⁿ† *yeoman*	47
John Hayne } *vnder xvj*			
Josias Hayne } *yeares of age.*		Thomas Noyce *his sonne*	15
Suffrance Hayne } *their*		Eliz: Noyce *his daughter*	
Mary Hayne } *daughters*			

---

* *Sutton Manfield*, then; and I think, now, *Sutton Mandeville.*   † *Southampton.*

Robert Dauis } his 30
John Rutter } seruantes 22
Margarett Dauis } 26

Nicholas Guy of Upton Gray,
in the County of Southⁿ,
Carpent'r 50
Jane Guy *his wife* 30
Mary Guy *his daughter*
Joseph Taynter } seruants 25
Robert Bayley } 23

John Bent of Penton* in the
County of Southⁿ *Husband-
man* 35
Martha Bent *his wife*
Robert Bent }
William Bent } *their Children*
Peter Bent } *all vnder ye age*
John Bent } *of xij yeares*
Ann Bent }

Roger Porter of Long Sut-
ton in the County of Southⁿ
Husbandm 55
Joane Porter }
Susan Porter } *his daughters*
Mary Porter }
Rose Porter }

John Sanders of Lanford† in
the County of Wilts, *Hus-
bandman* 25
Sara Sanders *his wife*
John Cole 40
Roger Easmen } 25
Richard Blake } seruants 16
William Cottle } 12
Robert King } 24

John Roaff of Melchitt‡ Parke
of Wilsheir *Husbandman* 50
Ann Roaff *his wife*
Hester Roaff *their daughter*
Thomas Whittle *their seruant* 18

John Goodenowe of Semley
in Wilsheir *Husbandman* 42
Jane Goodenowe *his wife*
Lydia Goodenowe } *their*
Jane Goodenowe } *daughters*

Edmvnd Goodenowe of Dun-
head in Wilsheire *Hus-
bandman* 27
Ann Goodenowe *his wife*
John Goodenowe } *their*
Thomas Goodenowe } *sonns 4*
} *yeares*
} *and vnder*
Richard Sangar *his seruant* 18

Thomas Goodenowe of Shas-
bury§ 30
Jane Goodenowe *his wife*
Thomas Goodenowe *his sonne* 1
Vrsula Goodenowe *his sister*

Edmvnd Kerley } of Ashmore 22
William Kerley } *Husbandmen*

Edmvnd Morres, of Keniton
Magna in Dorsetsh^r *Carpenter*

Stephan Kent of England|| 17
Margery Kent *his wife* 16
George Churche } 16
Hugh Marche } seruants 20
Anthony Sadler } 9

---

* There were then *Penton Grafton* and *Penton Mewsey*.   † *Langford*.

‡ *Millchill Park*. Incidentally mentioned, and by only one Topographer that I have consulted.

§ *Shaftesbury*, probably, in Dorsetshire.

|| Rather an indefinite locality for so young a couple, but such is the record.

THE FOUNDERS OF NEW ENGLAND.   59

Nicholas Wallington, *a poore boy*
Rebecca Kent, *seruant* 16
———
John Stephens ⎫ of Goñ-
William Stephens ⎬ sham* in 31
 ⎭ Oxon^r 21
husbandmen
Eliza: Stephens *his wife*
Alice Stephens *his Mother*
John Lowgie ⎫ *seruants* 16
Grace Lowgie ⎭
———
Thomas Jones of Goñsham
 p^r *Tayler* 36
Ann Jones *his wife*
Four Children vnder x yeeres.
William Baunsh ⎫ *seruants* 24
Jude Donley ⎭
———
Martha Wild^r of Shiplocket† in
 Oxfords^r *spinster*
Mary Wild^r *her Daughter*
Augustin Bearce 20
John Keene 17
Martha Keene 60
Eliza: Keene 13
Martha Keene
Josias Keene

Sara Keene
———
John Binson of Coñsham‡ in
 Ox: *husbandman* 30
Mary Binson *his wife*
John Binson ⎫ *their children*
Mary Binson ⎭ *vnder* 4 *yeares*
———
William Ilsbey ⎫ *shoemakers* 26
John Ilsbey ⎭
Barbara Ilsbey *his wife* 20
Phillip Dauis *his seruant* 12
———
Joseph Parker of Newbury
 Tanner 24
———
Sarah Osgood of Horrell,§
 spinster
Four children.
William Osgood ⎫ *children vn-*
William Jones ⎭ *der xj years*
Margery Parke *seruant*
———
John Ludwell 50
Henry Hangert ⎫ *seruants* 40
David Whealer ⎭ 11
———
Richard Bidgood, of Romsey,
 m^rchant

 The number of the passengers aforementioned, greate and little, are
Cx soules. Tho: Wurfres Coll and Ser^r
 Hen: Champante Cust^r
 N. Dingley Compt^r

[*Endorsement.*]—SO^uTHTON, 1638. The Cert. and List of the

———

* Perhaps *Godestow.* I find no *Goñsham,* early or late. There is also *Godington* or *Goddington,* a little to the N. E. of *Bicester. Godestow* is the site of an ancient Nunnery and is now included in *Woolvercott,* a mile N. of Oxford.
† *Shiplake,* by the Thames, two miles south of Henley.
‡ Doubtless the same place before named—*Goñsham.*
§ There is a *Horil* in Hamshire, near Linington.

Passeng^{rs} names gone for New-England in the Confidence of London in Aprill 1638.

SOUTHAMPTON.—The list of the names of Passeng^{rs} Intended to shipe themselues, In the Beuis* of Hampton of CL. Tounes, Robert Batten M^r for Newengland, And thus by vertue of the Lord Treasurers warrant of the second of May wch was after the restraynt and they some Dayes gone to sea Before the Kinges Mat^{es} Proclamacon Came vnto South'ton.

No. of persons.		Ages.
5†	John ffrey,‡ of Basing,§ *whelwrite* ; his wife and three children.	
4	Richard Austin, *tayler* (of Bishopstocke ;§) his wife and two children	40
1	Robert Knight, his seruant, *Carpenter*.	
8	{ Christopher Batt, of Sarum, *Tanner*	37
	Anne [Batt] *his wife*	32
	Dorothie Batt, there sister, and fiue children vnder tenne yeares	20
3	{ Thomas Good‖	24
	Eliza: Blackston } *servts*	22
	Rebecca Pond	18
8	{ William Carpenter } of Horwell¶ *Carpent^{re}*	62
	William Carpenter, Jun.	33
	Abigael Carpenter and fower children 10 and vnder	32
	Tho: Banshott, *servt*	14
9	{ Annis Littlefield and six children	38
	John Knight, *Carpenter*	
	Heugh Durdal	
4	{ Henery Byley of Sarū *tanner*	26
	Mary Byley	22
	Tho: Reeues, *servt*	
	John Byley	20
42		

---

* There is an ancient Legend of "Sir Bevis of Southampton." A mount in the neighborhood still bears the name of Beavis' Mount.

† Against some of the families or parties no number is set in the original—omitted, doubtless, in the hurry of business. I have supplied them.

‡ Settled at Andover, Mass. See Pedigree, Register, iii, 226. He and his sons spelled their names Fric. Their descendants changed it to Fry and Frye. J. W. D.

§ In Hampshire.

‖ A little uncertain, as the two last letters are blotted.

¶ Probably *Horil*.

42

⎧ Richard Dum{r} of New england	.	.	.	.	.	- 40
⎪ Alce Dum{r} ·	.	.	.	.	.	- 35
⎪ Tho: Dum{r} ·	.	.	.	.	.	- 19
⎪ Joane: Dum{r}	.	.	.	.	.	- 19
9 ⎨ Jane Dum{r} ·	.	.	.	.	.	- 10
⎪ Steephen Dum{r} *husbandman*	.	.	.	.	.	
⎪ Dorathie Dum{r}	.	.	.	.	.	- 6
⎪ Richard Dum{r}	.	.	.	.	.	- 4
⎩ Tho: Dum{r}	.	.	.	.	.	- 2

⎧ John Huchinson *Carpenter*	.	.	. ⎫	.	.	- 30
⎪ ffrauncis Alcocke *vizg*	.	.	. ⎪	.	.	- 26
⎪ Adam Moll, *tayler*	.	.	. ⎪	.	.	- 19
⎪ Will. Wackefeild	.	.	. ⎪	.	.	- 22
10 ⎨ Nathaunel Parker of London *Backer*	.	⎬ *Servants*	.	- 20
⎪ Samuel Poore	.	.	. ⎪	.	.	- 18
⎪ Da'yell Poore	.	.	. ⎪	.	.	- 14
⎪ Alce Poore ·	.	.	. ⎪	.	.	- 20
⎪ Richard Bayley ·	.	.	. ⎪	.	.	- 15
⎩ Anne Wackefield	.	.	. ⎭	.	.	- 20

61

The nomb{r} of the passeng{rs} aboue mentioned are Sixtie and one Soules.

Tho: Wurfres* Coll. and Sear{r}

Hen: Champante Cust{r}

D. Dingley Compt{r}

[*Endorsement.*]—Soũthton, 1638. The Cert. and list of the Passeng{rs} names gone for New England in the Bevis of Hampton, in May, 1638.

THE FOUNDERS OF NEW ENGLAND.

[Several Papers of the following description may serve to show that after 1638 a different system prevailed with relation to Emigrants leaving England for America.]

Whereas the Merchants Masters and Owners of the ship the Neptune haue by their Petition presented to the Board, being desirous to send the said shipp for New Englend, and from thence to Newfound land, and so to

---

* I have disposed these names, in every instance, as they stand upon the original papers, and spelled them as they are spelt.

Spaine, for wines to bring for Bristoll and having fraighted her with Passengers and Prouisions as are here vnder written can not bee permitted by the officer of the Custome in that Port, to put to Sea w^{th}out speciall order from the Bord. Did therefore this day Order that the Lo: high Treas. of England should bee hereby pleased and required forth^{th} to giue direcon to the officers of his Maties Customes there quietly to permit and suffer the said Marchants, master or owners to clere the said shipp the Neptune together with the number of passingers and the prouisions hereafter following, or so much thereof as his lp. in his judgment. shall find fitt; and that the Oaths of Allegiance, and Supremacy may be taken by all the passengers at Croconpill, by the officer appointed for that seruice as is vsual in like cases.

125 Passengers	2 Tonns of wine
150 barrells of beefe	100 gallons of Oyle
40 hogsheds of Mault	10,000 nayles
40 hogsheds of meale	one tonne and a half of strong water
150 dozen of stockens	
150 dozen of shooes	10 dozen of hatts
150 suits of Clothes	4 barrells of powder
150 dozen of shirts	20 musketts
150 dozen of drauers	500 weight of small shott
20 dozin Monmouth Capps	15 hogsheads of oatemeale
200 ells of cloth to make shirts	10 hogsheads of pease
20 pounds worth of iron tooles	250 weight of pewter
1000 weight of candles	500 weight of Sope
20 dozen of Bootes	2 Tonnes of vineger

[*Endorsement* :—] 17° Jan. 1639. Order for ye Neptune to goe wth passengers and Provisions to New England. Ent.

[I have met with but four papers of this description in my researches in the British Archives, and these are in Her Majesty's State Paper office. Thinking they might be interesting to the student in early New England history, I have transcribed them for this work. Besides showing what commodities were then in greatest demand in that country, it is also shown that not much more trouble was taken by the government about Emigrants than any other part of the cargo; as, for aught that can now be found, not even a list of the names of those were taken. Nor does it appear, that they were not sworn to *Allegiance* and *Supremacy* in *a lot.*

The form to each of these three lists or shipments of merchandize being the same, those forms to the other two lists are omitted. In the heading of the next form is, however, this addition :—" The Merchants, owners, &c. of the ship Fellowship of Bristol, sent the said ship the last year from that Port to New England laden with Passengers and Provisions, and from thence to New found land, and laded fish wch they carried to Malligo in Spaine, and there sould it, lading her from thence back to Bristoll wth wines, and paid his Matie great Sumes of money for the Customes thereof." Then the form proceeds as in the last.]

250 Passingers	40 tonne of wyne
300 Barrells of Beef	200 gallons of oyle
80 hogsheads of Mault	20,000 of nayles
80 hogsheads of meale	3 tonns of strong water
300 dozn. of stockings	20 dozn. of Hatts
300 dozen of shoes	8 barrells of powder
300 suits of clothes	40 Muskets
300 dozn. of shirts	1000 weight of small shott
300 dozen. of drauers	30 hogsheads of oatmeale
40 dozen. of Monmouth Capps	20 hogsheads of pease
400 ells of cloth to make shirts	500 weight of pewter
40 pounds worth of iron tooles	1000 weight of Sope
2000 weight of Candles	2 tonn's of viniger.

[*Endorsement* :—] 17 Jan. 1639. Order for 2 ships of Bristoll to goe to New England with passengers and provisions. Ent.

[The third of these documents is as follows :—]

17 Jan. 1639. Whereas George Foxcroft and other Merchants trading to New England, Spane, &c. and the owners of the shipp Desire of Newengland did by their Pet^n represent that haueing Estates lying in Newengland aforesaid, in Clapboards pipe staues, hoopes, fish and other comodities, and intending to buy fish in the Newfound land to transtport into Spaine and other places ;—humbly besought the Boord that they might be permitted not only to proceed wth their said shipp in this voyage, but haue leaue to take in and carry such passengers and provisions for New England as shalbe offered, without wch helpe they can not proceed in their intencōns nor possesse themselues of their Estates in new England ;

W^{ch} their Wps taking into consideracoñ, did think fitt and this day Order &c. as before.]

  50 passengers   20 quarters Oats and Oat meale
  15 firkins Butter   150 quarters Mault and Barly
  10 C waight Cheese   10 Barrills Powder
  20 hoghd. Beefe   10 thousand Biskett
  10 hoghd. Pork   40 Barrills tallow and suet
  30 quarters Wheat and wheat   200 dozn. shooes
    meale   10 dozn. Bootes
  20 quarters Rye and Rye   20 quarters Pease
    meale   50 hundred weight Candles.

The like Order for the ship called the William and George wth the Prouisions following, first

  180 passengers.

[Then follows the invoice of merchandize, which being composed of the same items as those already copied, is omitted.]

[*Endorsement* :—]   17° Januarij, 1639. Order for 2 Ships to carry Passengers and Provisions to New England. Ent.

EMIGRANTS FOR ST. CHRISTOPHERS.

[Among a mass of MSS. exhibited to me in the Rolls Office, there was a very little book, with a vellum cover, about four by five inches, and containing but six leaves. The outside of the cover is thus inscribed :—]

" The Names of such as passed out of the poart of Plimworth Ano Dme 1634."

[What follows is an entire copy of the whole book.]

Plymouth ffebr: 1633. Passengers in the Robert Bonaventure for St Christophers

   George fford of Exoñ,* aged 30 yeares.
   Stephen Whittington, of Lincolne, 20 yeares.
   John Thomas of St. Tiffey,† 26 yeres.
   John Liddicott of St. Cullum,‡ 22.

---

* Exeter.   † Perhaps St. Teath in Cornwall.
‡ Probably Columb in Cornwall.

Wm Clarke of Truro, 20.
Tho: ffrethy of Perintho,* 24.
Michaell Bowden of Holston, 27.
John Badland of Northill, 22.
Richard Slavelie of Stoñehowse, 40
Richard Cocke of Wincklye, 33
Henry Rensby of St. Stephens, 28
Anthony Webb of Lanceston, 20
Gregory Sam of Chidleigh, 15
Christopher Carter of St. Gilt, 45
Martin Rooby of Guindiron, 23
Wm. Curke of Monteratt, 24
Henry Thomas of Luxulian, 15
Stephen Symon of Plimpton, 18
Mathew Arthur of Plimpton, 18
Jane Trewin of Plimpton, aged 26 yeares.
Wm Johnson of London,   32   "
Reignold ffrost of Tottnes, 15
John ffarren of Peter Tauey, 2
Wm Wade of Bodmin, 33
Nichās Dabbin of St. Stephens, 40
Andrew Picke of Great Dalby, 34
John Penington of Symon Ward, 40
Tho Pollard of Paranenth, 23
Ellin Nauearro of Penryn, 20
Rawleigh Edye of Bodmyn, 15
Wm Dun of Truro, 16
Anth: Pearse of St. Breage, 16
Edward Trennueere of Helston, 18
Robt: Treneeghau, of Helston, 34
Tego Leaue of Corke in Ireland, 30
    Rec. for these:
All husbandmen bound to serve here, some 3 and some 4 yeares.

---

* Perhaps Peramthon in Cornwall.

1633.   1° mcij.   In the Margarett for St. Christophers

Thomas Roseter of Washboro, 20 yeares.
Tho: Martin of Cardinham, 24
John Dustan, of St. Cullom, 26
Richard Williams of St. Cullom, 30
John Newdon of St. Tue, 28
Anth: Burrowes of Jacobstow, 20
Robert Oliver of Crediton, 20
Barth: Cornew: of Crediton, 18
Clement Barry of Exon, 22.
ffrancis Pedler of St. Breage, 28
Robt Pedler of St. Breage, 22
John Merry of Withiell, 28
Walter Burlace of Luggom, 22
Samuell fforgine of Wallen Lizard, 26
Richard Edward of St Virian, 28
Richard Symondes of Wantage, 28
Robt Paine of Marrozun, 29
Wm Badcocke of St. Hillary, 20
Simon Martin of St. Ives, 18
George Griffin of Marazion, 18
Tho: Sleman of St. Hillary, 18
John Sanders of Marozion, 18
Thomas Borinthon of Helston, 22
Wm Writt, of Marozion, 17
Nichas Warerman or [of] Marozion, 15
Samuell Purefoy of St. Ives, 13.
George Mathew of Ludswan, 23
Teage Williams, Irishman, 18
    Rect. for them   0^{li} 15^s 0^d

All husbandmen for the most pt as the former.

                                        Joseph Boole
                                         is Debuta ther.

[Here follows the whole of another book, similar in size and form to the last named:—]

A list of the names and surnames of those psons wch are bound for St Christoph^{r} and haue taken the oath of Allegiance before me Mr William Gourney, Maior of Dartmouth, they being brought before me the twentyeth day of ffebruary in ye yeare of o^{r} Lord god 1634.

Imprimis William Haukins, of Exoñ, Glouer, aged 25 yeares or there abouts.

James Courtney, of Exoñ, A Blacksmith Aged 23 yeares or thereabouts.

Richard Skose of Newton Abbot, A Seafaringe Man, 37 yeares or thereabouts.

Francis Boyce of London, a Button hole maker, aged 25 yeares or thereabouts.

William Carkille, of Plimouth, a Saylemaker, aged 21 yeares or thereabouts.

William Gurge, of Exoñ, a shoemaker, aged 20 yeares or thereabouts.

Alce Whitmor, of Huniton in Devon, Spinster, aged 25 yeares or thereabouts.

Philipp Stephens of Ashbertan in Devon, Spinster, aged 28 yeares or thereabouts.

Sara Coose of Exoñ Spinster, aged 18 years or therabouts.

Judith Stevens of Exoñ, Spinster, aged 19 years or therabouts.

Margarett Harwood, of Stokegabriell in Devon, Spinster, aged 22 yeares or thereabouts.

Edward Morris, of Exoñ a Locker, aged 21 yeares or thereabouts.

Thomas Bryant of Bampton in Devonshire, a husbandman aged 23 years or therabouts.

Willyam May of Maymard in Somersett, a sea man aged 32 yeares or therabouts.

Hulinne Oneth, of St. Stevens in Cornwall, a husbandman, aged 34.

John Wille in Barnstable in Devon a ffeltmaker, Aged 35 years or therabouts.

Symon Weeks, of Exoñ, a Worsted weaver, aged 16 yeares or thereabouts.

Thomas Jermayne of Exoñ, an Ostler, aged 30 years.

John ffrench, of Washford in Ireland, a Seaman, 26 years.

Willen Bill of Great Torington in Devonshire, a husbandman, aged 28 yeares.

John Hocksley, of Stoke Cannon in Devon, a Taylor, aged 28 years.
James Ruosman, of London, a husbandman, aged 21 years.
Elizabeth Reed, of Exon, a spinster, aged 19 years or therabouts.
Mary Harte, of Lyme, a spinster, aged 18 years or therabouts.
Mary Hoppine, of Exmister, a spinster, aged 20 years.
Mary Harries of Stoke Pomneroy in Devon, aged 23 years or therabouts.
Elizabeth Quicke, of Barnstable in Devon, aged 18 years.
Elizabeth Hill of Brixam in Devon, aged 24 years.
Joane Shorte of Exon, Aged 20 years.
Joane Lauere, of Modbury in Devon, aged 19 years.
Jane Gouldinge of St. Thom: the Apostle in Devon, aged 16 years or therabouts.

James Worthy Deputy
for Mr Thoroughgood.

[The following list is from a paper without date. The Capt. *Hopson* mentioned in it is the Capt. *Hobson* of the New England Histories, probably.]

A List of Sea Men's Names wch Capt. John Hopson one of his Maties Councell in Virgenia desireth to be exempted from ye presse in Regarde of his Present intended Voyage of Virginia in ye good shipp called ye Vnity of ye Isle of Wyghte.

William Vpton, M^r:	Nicholas Sallter
Richard White, Mate	Nicholas Godfrie
William Godfrie	John Persie
William Minterne	William Oden
William Poul	John Orchard
Thomas Wooden	John Smith
Thomas Wise	John Preston.
Robert Carter	*Her Maj. St. P. Office.*

PASSENGERS IN THE MARY AND JOHN, 1634.

[The following very important List of Passengers was communicated to the Editor by the Hon. George Lunt of Boston, and was published in the New England Historical and Genealogical Register for July, 1855. Mr. Lunt says " he received it through Mr. Cleveland of Salem." It supplies "a gap long bewailed in the early history of Newbury, as it comprises many well-known names of residents of that town and its vicinity," who were the original founders of numerous families still bearing the same names there and elsewhere in New England.

The following extract from the Records of the Council of State will show from what tyranny our fathers escaped in their native land.]

New England.—At White Hall the last of Feb: 1633.
Present
  Lo. Arch Bp. of Cant. [William Laud.]*
  Lo. Keeper. [Sir Thomas Coventry.]
  Lo. Privie Seal. [Henry Montague, Earl of Manchester.]
  Lo. High Chamberline. [Robert Bertie, Lord Willoughby of Eresby.†
  Earle of Kelly. [Thomas Erskine, first Earl.]
  Lo. [Francis] Cottington.
  Mr. V. Chamb'line. [Sir Thomas Jermyn, Kt.]
  Mr. Compt'. [Sir Henry Vane, Sen.]
  Mr. Secretary. [Sir Francis] Wyndibank.

Whereas by Warr^t bearing date 22nd of this Present the sev^{r}all ships following bound for New England & now lying in the River of Thames were made staye of untill further order from their L'opps Viz^t. the Clement & Job, The Reformation, The True Loue, The Elizabeth Bonadventure, The Sea Flower, The Mary & John, The Planter, The Elizabeth & Dorcas, The Hercules & the Neptune.

For as much as the Masters of the said ships were this day called before the Board & several Particulars given them in charge to be performed in their said Voyage, amongst which the said Masters were to enter into several Bonds of One Hundred Pounds a piece to His Maj^{s}tys use before the Clarke of the Councell attendant to observe & cause to be observed & putt in Execuc'on these Articles following vizt.

1. That all & every Person aboard their Ships now bound for New England as aforesaid, that shall blaspheme or profane the Holy name of God be severely punish't.

---

* He had not been a year in his high office. Geo. Abbot whom he succeeded, died 4 Aug. 1633.
† Killed in the battle of Edge Hill, 23 October, 1642.

2. That they cause the Prayers contained in the Book of Common Prayers establisht in the Church of England to be said daily at the usual hours for Morning & Evening Prayers & that they cause all persons aboard their said Ships to be present at the same.

3. That they do not receive aboard or transport any person that hath not Certificate from the Officers of the Port where he is to imbarque that he hath taken both the Oathes of Alleigeance & Supremacy.

4. That upon their return into this Kingdom they Certify to the Board the names of all such Persons as they shall transport together with their Proceedings in the Execuc'on of the aforesaid Articles—Whereunto the said M^{rs} have conformed themselves—It was therefore & for divers other Reasons best known to their Lo^{pps} thought fitt that for this time they should be permitted to proceed on their Voyage, and it was thereupon Ordered that Gabriel Marsh Esqr. Marshalle of the Admiralty & all other His Maj'tys Officers to whom their said Warr^t was directed should be required upon Sight hereof to discharge all & every the said Ships & Suffer them to depart on their intended Voyage to New England.

Ex^t. JON MEANTYS.

The names of such Passengers as took the Oathes of Supremacy, & Alleigeance to pass for New England in the Mary & John of London Robert Sayres master.

24th Mar 1633	Richard Jacob	William White
William Trace	Daniel Ladd	Matthew Hewlett *Her-*
John Marshe	Robert Kingsman	John Wheyler [*cules*
John Luff	John Bartlett	William Clarke
Henry Traske	Robert Coker	Robert Neuman
William Moudey	William Savery	Adrian Vincent
Robert Sever	John Anthony, Left	
Thomas Avery	behind	The 26th day of March.
Henry Travers	Stephen Jurden	Nicholas Easton
Thomas Sweete	John Godfrey	Richard Kent
John Woodbridge	George Browne	Abraham Mussey
Thomas West	Nicholas Noyce	William Ballard
Thomas Savery	Richard Browne	Matthew Gillett
Christopher Osgood	Richard Reynolds	William Franklin
Philip Fowler	Richard Littlehall	John Mussey

Thomas Cole	Henry Shorte	William Newbey
Thomas Parker	William Hibbens	Henry Lunt
James Noyce	Richard Kent	Joseph Pope
John Spencer	Joseph Myles	Thomas Newman
William Spencer	John Newman	John Newman

For which we gave certificate, together with five others wh^{ch} are said to be left behind to oversee the Chattle to pass in the Hercules vizt.

The names of the Passengers in the Hercules of London, John Kiddey Ma^r: for New England—

These six Passengers took their Oathes of Supremacy & Alleigeance the 24th of March and were left behind the Mary & John as intended to pass in ye Hercules—Viz^t.

John Anthoney
Robert Early
William Latcome } Cert. the six first to Mt'er Sayers as intended
Thomas Foster   Secondh to Mr Kiddey to pass in the Her-
William Foster cules—
Matthew Hewlett

16th April 1634—Nathaniel Davyes
George Kinge
Thomas Rider
William Elliott
William Fifeilde
18 Henry Phelps—

These Proceedings were Copyed out of an Olde Book of Orders belonging to the Port of South'ton but now remaining at the Custom house in Portsmouth the 6th Day of December 1735—

p^r THOMAS WHITEHOUSE.

[The following items were communicated by Mr. Horatio G. Somerby, and published in the New England Historical and Genealogical Register for October, 1848. They are from the same source as those in the previous pages.]

29 August William Norton xxv yeres old is to transport himself to New
1635   England & to imbarque himself in the Hopewell p. cert:
        from the minister of his conformitie to the church discipline

	of England: he hath taken the oath of Allegeance & Supremacie. Die et A° pred.
5 September 1635	Thomas Turner of age XLII yeres to passe to New England imbarqued in the Hopewell hath brought Certificate of his Conformitie & tooke the oath of Allegeance & Supremacie

       (Signed)   Thomas Turner.

8 Sept. 1635.	Robert Pennaire of age 21 yeres & Tho: Pennaire X yeres old are to imbarque in Mr. Babb bound to New England have brought certificate from Doctor Denison of his conformitie. He hath taken the oath of Allegeance & Suprem.
4 Sept. 1635.	Robert Edwards 27 yeres who is to pass to Virginia hath hath taken the oath of Allegeance

       (Signed)   Robert Edwards.

1635	Tho: Bigmore aged 34 dwelling in New England Fether Seller to pass to Amsterdam on his affairs.

SCOTCH PRISONERS SENT TO MASSACHUSETTS IN 1652, BY ORDER OF THE ENGLISH GOVERNMENT.

[From the first volume of the Registry of Deeds, Boston, County of Suffolk.]

[The following extract from Hutchinson's *Collection of Original Papers* doubtless has reference to some Prisoner Passengers in the same situation as those whose names are here given. The extract is from a letter of Mr. John Cotton, minister of Boston, to Lord General Cromwell, dated " Boston, N. Eng., 28 of the 5th, 1651." This letter having been written before the arrival of these prisoners, could not refer to them, although they may have been among those taken at Dunbar. That battle was fought September 3, 1650.

" The Scots, whom God delivered into your hands at Dunbarre, and whereof sundry were sent hither, we have been desirous (as we could) to make their yoke easy. Such as were sick of the scurvy or other diseases have not wanted physick and chyrurgery. They have not been sold for slaves to perpetual servitude, but for 6 or 7 or 8 yeares, as we do our owne; and he that bought the most of them (I heare) buildeth houses for them, for every four an house, layeth some acres of ground thereto, which he giveth them as their owne, requiring 3 dayes in the weeke to worke for him (by turnes) and 4 dayes for them themselves, and promiseth, as soone as they can repay him the money he layed out for them, he will set them at liberty."]

London, this 11 : of Nouember 1651 :
Mr Tho: Kemble

Wee whose names are vnder written, freighte^{rs} of the sh[ipp] John & Sara whereof is Comander John Greene Doe Consigne the said shipp & servants to be disposed of by yow for ou^r best Advantage & account & the whole proceed of the Servants & vojage Retourne in a jojnct stocke without any Division in such goods as you conceive will turne best to acco^{nt} in the Barbadoes & consign[e] them to M^r. Charles Rich for the aforesajd acco^{tt} & w^t other pay yo^w meete with fit for this place send hither & take the Advise & Asistance of Capt J^{no} Greene in disposall of the Servants Dispatch of the shipp or w^t else may any wajes concerne the vojage thus wishing the shipp a safe vojage & God's blessing on the same not doubting of you^r best care & diligence, Remajne :

Signatum et Recognitum in p^r ncja   you^r loving freinds Jo: Beex
   Jo: Nottock notarius publ: Robt Rich
                                              Wiljam Greene

Entred & Recorded at the Instant Request of the said Mr Tho: Kemble.
p^r Edw: Rawson Recorder 13th May 1652.

London this 11th: of Nouember, 1651 :
Capt. J^{no}: Greene

Wee whose names are vnder written freighte^{rs} of you^r shipe the John & Sara doe Order yow forthwith as winde & weather shall permitt to sett sajle for Boston in New England & there deliver our Orders and Servants to Tho: Kemble of charles Toune to be disposed of by him according to orde^{rs} wee have sent him in that behalfe & wee desire yow to Advise with the sajd Kemble about all that may concerne that whole Jntended vojage vsing you^r Jndeavo's with the sajd Kemble for the speediest lading you^r shipp from New Eng: to the barbadoes with provisions & such other things as are in N. E. fitt for the West Indjes where yow are to deliuer

74   THE FOUNDERS OF NEW ENGLAND.

them to Mr. Charles Rich to be disposed of by him for the Joinct acco^{nt} of the freighte^rs & so to be Retou'ned home in a stocke vndevided thus desiring your Care & industrje in Dispatch and speed of the vojage wishing you a happy & safe Retourne wee Remajne you^r loving freinds

    Signatum et Recognitum   John Beex
      in p'ncia : Jo : Nottock : notar Publ :   Robt. Rich
    13 May 1652.   Will. Greene

        Entred & Recorded p^r Edward Rawson Recorde^{r.}

A LIST OF THE PASSENGERS ABOARD THE JOHN AND SARAH OF LONDON JOHN GREENE MR BOUND FOR NEW ENGLAN[D]

Donald Roye	Wm Banes	Patrick Jimson
James Moore	Patrick Jones	John Hanoman
Walter Jackson	Andrew Wilson	Andrew Jerris
Michaell ffossem	Daniell Monwilliam	James Jackson
Daniell Simson	John Mackenthow	Patricke Tower
John Rosse	John Jamnell	Wm Mackannell
Sander Milleson	David Mackhome	Dani: Mackajne
Daniell Monlow	Murtle Mackjlude	Senly Mackonne
Henry Brounell	Salamon Sinclare	James English
James farfason	John Gurden	Dan: Mackennell
Alester lowe	Wm Macken	John Mackey
Daniell Hogg	John Cragon	Danniell Gunn
Hugh Mackey	John Graunt	James Ross
Daniell Mackannell	Alestre Mackrore	John Wilson
John Croome	Daniell Mackendocke	David Jeller
John Macklude	Gellust Mackwilliam	George Quenne
Dan: Mackwell	James Milward	John Jenler
**** Mackunnell	Wm Dell	John Woodell
John Hudson	James Micknab	George Perry
John Mackholme	Glester Macktomas	John Monrow
John Beme	Almister Mackalinsten	Wm Clewston
**** More	John Coehon	Daniell Mackhan
John Crag	Robe^rt Jenler	Alester Mackhene
Robe^rt Monrow	Edward Dulen	Alester Simson
Hill Mackie	John Hogg	Richard Jackson
John Mackdonell	James Mickell	James Camell
Allester Macknester	John Mackalester	Dan: Martjn
John Edminsteire	Daniell Macknell	John Hogg

John Robinson
John Rosse
John Rosse
Hugh Monrow
Thomas Bereere
Sjmon Russell
John Morre
Edward Punn
Sannder Morrot
Wm ffresell
John Boye
John Buckanen
Patricke Morton
Danell Makalester
James Michell
Sander Mackdoell
James Gurner
Wm Teller
Origlais Mackfarson
Nicholas Wallis
John Murrow
Robert Highen
John Mackhellin
Allester *****
Dan: Mackhellin
***** *****
Charles Lesten
Wm Stewart
John Morre
Edward ffressell
David Hinne
Daniell blacke
Daniell Sessor
Patricke Mackatherne
Alexandr Tompson
Danell Kemper
Daniell How
John Brow*
Sam Shiva***
Henry Mack***
John Robinson
Daniel *****
Patricke *****

Patricke *****
P**** *****
***** *****
***** [Mac]kfarson
***** Macklyne
***** Monrow
***ster Macknell
Daniell Robinson
[J]ames Shone
John Anderson
James Graunt
Patricke Crosshone
John Grant
John Scott
Dan: Gordon
Dan: Ross
John Hogg
Patrick Mann
Ansell Sherron
James Ross:
David Hamilton
Patricke Mackneile
David Ross:
Amos Querne
Alestre Hume
Neile Johnson
Alester Rallendra
Rory Hamilton
James Robinson
David Buckanon
David Sterling
Daniell Macknith
Robt Mackfarson
Wm Munckrell
Neile Camell
Sennell Mackneth
John Mackane
Dan Shuron
Rory Machy
Patricke Graunt
Patricke Harron
James Rowe
Sander Simson

James Gorden
Charles Robinson
Alester Robinson
Patricke Robertson
Alester graunt
Neile Macketh
Patricke Macknith
Daniell Macknith
James Hedeicke
James Mackhell
John Curmickhell
David Hume
Patrick Macktreth
David Anderson
Wm Beames
David Monwilljam
John Sterling
John Mann
Wm Dengell
Daniell Mann
Sander Mackcunnell
Cana Mackurnall
Patricke Mackane
Ansell Sotherland
Sander Miller
James Pattison
Alexander Graunt
Thomas Graunt
Neile Carter
Dan: Mackneile
John Shenne
Robt Mackajne
Dan: Hudson
Neile Murrow
John Cannell
Evan Tiler
Jonas Murrow
Alester Mackhele
Edward Dengle
James Kallender
Jonas Ross
Neile Mackone
James Graunt

David Tenler	David Jameson	Henry Smith
James Mackally	Dan: Simson	Wm Hidrecke
Wm Mackajne	George Hame	Cana Macktentha
Alester Tooth	James Crockford	Niele Hogg
Austin Stewart	David Kallender	Robt Mackhane
Laughlell Montrosse	David Patterson	Robt Stewart
Wm Mackontoss	Alester Anderson	David Simson
Neile Mackajne	Patricke Smison	Laughleth Gordon
James Mackreith	Robt: Boy	Neile Jameson
John Mackforsen	John Wilson	Patrick English
James Hamilton	Patricke Jacson	James Benne
John Graunt	Wm Mackajne	David Milward
James Murrow	Dan: Mackhoe	Wm Anderson
Wm Carmackhell	Dan: Mackajne	Sander Mackey
James Mackneile	Alester Ross	Patrick Sotherland
Samuell Mackajne	Neile Muckstore	Daniel Oneale
Dan: Graunt	Wm Mackandra	John Woodall
Cha: Stewart	John Boye	Christopher Wilson
Neile Stewart	Wm Graunt	John Murrow
David Macketh	James Graunt	

The persons afore named passed from hence in the ship aforementioned and are according to order Registed heare.

Dat. Search office, Grauesend 8th· Nouember, 1651.

GILES BARROW ⎫
EDW: PELLING ⎬ Searchers.
JOHN MORRIS ⎭

Jn the Jn° & Sara of London John Greene m^r for New England:— Robt Rich m^{rt} Jronworke household stuffe & other p^rovisions for Plante^rs and scotch p^risone^rs free by ordinance of Parliament dat 20th of October 1651.

S
G R

No[•] two trusses of goods for plante^rs shipt the viiith of Nouember 1651 m^rkt & nombred as in the magent.

JOHN BEADLEY* Sc.   wth ye Armes of ye Comonwealth.
Entred & Recorded at the Request of m^r Thomas kemble. 14 May 1652

p^r EDWARD RAWSON Recorder.

---

* It is difficult to decide whether the above name is Beadley or Bradley, as in the chirography of Secretary Rawson the letters *e* and *r* are often made precisely alike.

"A LYST OF THE PASINGERS ABORD THE SPEEDWELL OF LONDON, ROBERT LOCK MASTER, BOUND FOR NEW ENGLAND.

[The original, of which the following is a copy, is in possession of the Editor.]

Richard Stratton,	aged		Shudrack Hopgood,	aged	14
John Mulfoot,	"		Thomas Goodynough,	"	20
Richard Smith,	"	43	Nathaniel Goodinough,	"	16
Francis Brinsley,	"	22	John Fay,	"	8
Thomas Noyce,	"	32	William Tayler,	"	11
Mathew Edwards,	"		Richard Smith,	"	28
Joseph Boules,	"	47	Muhuhulett Munnings,	"	24
William Brand, (Q) *	"	40	Margarett Mott,	"	12
John Copeland, (Q)	"	28	Henry Reeue,	"	8
Christopher Holder, (Q)	"	25	Henery Seker,	"	8
Thomas Thurston, (Q)	"	34	John Morse,	"	40
Mary Prince, (Q)	"	21	Nickolus Dauison,	"	45
Sarah Gibbons, (Q)	"	21	John Baldwin,	"	21
Mary Weatherhead, (Q)	"	26	Mary Baldwin,	"	20
Dorothy Waugh, (Q)	"	20	Rebeca Worster,	"	18
Lester Smith,	"	24	John Wigins,	"	15
Christopher Clarke,	"	38	John Miller,	"	24
Edward Lane,	"	36	Thomas Home,	"	11
Tho: Richardson	"	19	John Crane,	"	11
John Earle,	"	17	Charels Baalam,	"	18
Thomas Barnes,	"	20			

"The persons aboue named past from hence [in] the shipp aboue mentioned, and are, according to order, registred heare. Dated, Searchers office, Grauesend, 30th May, 1656.

EDWARD PELLING, } *Searchers.*
JOHN PHILPOTT,

"Theese were Landed at Boston in N. E. the 27th of the 6th moneth, 1656. J. E."

---

* The eight names against which is the letter Q had a Q set opposite to them in the margin of the original paper, denoting, as is supposed, that the individuals were Quakers. It is said in Sewall's History of the Quakers that there arrived at Boston two other Quakers in July of this year, namely, Mary Fisher and Ann Austin, who were very ill treated on their arrival, by Gov. Bellingham, though there was yet no law against Quakers.

PASSENGERS FOR NEW ENGLAND.

[From the original in the Editor's possession.]

1671. A List of the Names of the Passengers on board the Ship Arabella Richard Sprague Master for New England, May ye 27th, 1671.

William Shoars,	John Clarke,	Joseph Bortes,
William Hadwell,	Robert Halworthy,	Samuel Borthamer,
William Syton,	Eliza Coleman,	Robert Gibbert,
George Ash,	Andrew Rodgers,	Henry Mumford,
George Bearbeik,	Joseph Read,	Henry Tarlton,
Robert Collins,	Thomas Webb,	William Twide,
William Bently,	John Parker,	Cooleman.
Josiah Hobbs,	Stephen Bustells,	

Grauesend May 27th: 1671. The Passengers aboue mentioned were all willing to goe to New England as are Registered according to order.

William Burnney
Clarke of ye Passage

This is a True Coppie as attests Free Grace Bendall
Cleric.

DANIEL CUSHING'S RECORD.

DANIEL CUSHING of Hingham, one of the Founders of New England, left the following record of Norfolk emigrants. Mr. Cushing, we are told, in the excellent Address by Solomon Lincoln, Esq., on the two hundredth anniversary of the settlement of Hingham, " was conspicuous in the annals of that town, in various public offices, especially in those of Town Clerk and a Magistrate." He left among his papers an account of those emigrants, which is appended to Mr. Lincoln's Address. It had not before been printed. It was thought the propriety of admitting it here would not be questioned, and the Author of the Address being applied to, kindly allowed it to be added to the other lists in this work.

" A list of the names of such persons as came out of the town of Hingham, and Towns adjacent in the County of Norfolk, in the Kingdom of England, into New England, and settled in Hingham, in New England, most of them as followeth : —

1633. Imprimis, in the year of our Lord God 1633, Theophilus Cushing came from Hingham in Norfolk, and lived several years at Mr. Hains's (Hayne's) farm and many years before he dyed he lived at Hingham, in New England, and there he dyed, being about 100 years old, and was blind about 25 years of the said time.   1

1633. Edmond Hobart, senior, same from said Hingham, with his wife and his son Joshua and his daughters Rebekah and Sarah and their servant Henry Gibbs, into New England, and settled first at Charlestown and after, the said Edmond Hobart and his son Joshua and Henry Gibbs settled in this Town of Hingham.   3

Also Ralph Smith came from Old Hingham and lived in this town.   1

1633. Also Nicholas Jacob with his wife and two children, and their cosen Thomas Lincoln, weaver, came from Old Hingham, and settled in this Hingham.   4
   1

1633. Also Edmond Hobart and his wife came from Old Hingham, and settled in this Hingham.   2

1633. Also Thomas Hobart came from Windham, with his wife and 3 children, and settled in Hingham.   5

1634. Thomas Chubbuck and his wife came and settled in this Hingham.   2

1635. Mr. Peter Hobart Minister of the Gospell, with his wife and 4 children, came into New England, and settled in this town of Hingham, and was Pastor of the Church   years.   6

1635. Mr. Anthony Cooper with his wife and 4 sons and 4 daughters and 4 servants, came from Old Hingham, and settled in New Hingham.   14

1635. John Farrow and his wife and child came from Old Hingham, and settled in New Hingham.   3

1635. William Large and his wife came and settled at New Hingham.   2

Also George Ludkin his wife and son.   3

1637. John Tower and Samuel Lincoln came from Old Hingham, and both settled at New Hingham.   2

Samuel Lincoln living some time at Salem.

   —
   49

1638. Mr. Robert Peck preacher of the Gospell in the Town of Hingham, in the County of Norfolk, in Old England, with his wife and 2 children and two servants came over the sea, and settled in this Town of Hingham, and he was teacher of the Church. 6

1638. Mr. Joseph Peck and his wife with 3 sons and daughter, and 2 men servants and 3 maid servants came from Old Hingham and settled in New Hingham 10

1638. Edward Gillman, with his wife 3 sons and two daughters and 3 servants, came and settled in this Town of Hingham. 8

1638. John Foulsham and his wife and two servants, came from Old Hingham and settled in New Hingham. 4

1638. Henry Chamberlin shoe maker his wife and his mother and two children, came from Old Hingham and settled at New Hingham 5

1638. Steven Gates his wife and 2 children, came from Old Hingham, and settled in New Hingham. 4

_____

37

1638. George Knights his wife and child came from Barrow, and settled in New Hingham. 3

1638. Thomas Cooper and his wife and two children and two servants and two other persons (viz:) John Tufts and Robert Skouling, came from Old Hingham, and thereabout, and settled in New Hingham. 8

1638. Mathew Cushing and his wife and 4 sons and one daughter, and his wife's sister Frances Ricroft, widow came from Old Hingham and settled at New Hingham. 8

1638. John Beale, shoemaker, with his wife and 5 sons and 3 daughters and 2 servants, came from Old Hingham and settled at New Hingham. 12

1638. Elizabeth Sayer and Mary Sayer came from Old Hingham, and settled in New Hingham. 2

1638. Francis James and his wife and 2 servants (to witt) Thomas Sucklin and Richard Baxter came from Old Hingham and settled in New Hingham. 4

1638. Philip James his wife and 4 children and two servants (viz)

William Pitts and Edward Michell came from Old Hingham 8
and settled in New Hingham. Philip James dyed soon after
he came.

1638. James Buck with his servant John Morfield, came from Old 2
Hingham and settled in New Hingham.

1638. Also in the same ship that the above named persons came in,
came divers other persons out of several towns near to Old
Hingham, (viz :) Steven Paine with his wife and 3 sons 4 9
servants, came from Great Ellingham and settled in New
Hingham.

1638. John Sutton and his wife and four children came from Atle- 6
burraye, (Attleboro') and settled in New Hingham.

1638. Steven Lincoln and his wife and his son Steven, came from 3
Windham, and settled in New Hingham.

1638. Samuel Packer and his wife and child came from Windham,
and settled in New Hingham. 3

1638. Thomas Lincoln and Jeremiah Moore came from Windham,
and settled in New Hingham. 2

1638. Mr. Henry Smith and his wife and 3 sons and two daughters,
and three men servants, and 2 maid servants, and Thomas
Mayer came from Ha**en Hall in Norfolk, and settled in 13
New Hingham.

1638. Mr. Bozone Allen and his wife and two servants came from
Lynn, in Norfolk, and settled in New Hingham. 4
Also William Riply and wife and 4 children. 6

1638. Mathew Hawk and his wife, and his servant John Ferring,
came from Cambridge, in Old England, and settled in New
Hingham. 3

96

All the persons above named that came over in the year
1638, were 133, came in one ship called the Diligent of
Ipswich; the master was John Martin of said Ipswich. All
before named that came before were 42 persons. 133
42

175

All of them settled in this * * Town of Hingham.

1639. Edmond Pitts and his wife and child and his brother Leonard Pitts and Adam Foulsham, came from Old Hingham and settled in New Hingham. 5
Frances Ricroft died in a few weeks after she came; and Mr. Robert Peck his wife his son Joseph and his maid went to England again in the year 1641.

1638. William Riply and his wife and 2 sons and two daughters came from Old Hingham, and settled in New Hingham. 6

1635. John Smart and his wife and 2 sons, came out of Norfolk, in Old England, and settled in New Hingham. 4

1637. Henry Tuttil and his wife, and Isaac Wright, came out of Norfolk, and settled in New Hingham. 3

1637. William Ludkin, the Smith, and his wife came from Norwich, and settled in New Hingham. 2
—
1637. From * * * in Norfolk came John Cutler, and his wife 7   9
children one servant.   10
—
19

All the persons that came from Norfolk in Old England in several years (viz:) beginning to come in the year 1633, until the year and in the year 1639, were 206. The most of them came from Old Hingham, and the rest of them from several other towns thereabout and settled in this town of New Hingham."

EMIGRANTS* IN THE HERCULES OF SANDWICH,

Of 200 tons, John Witherley, master, bound for "the plantation called New England in America, with certificates from the ministers where they last dwelt, of their conversation, and conformity to the orders and discipline of the church, and that they had taken the oath of allegiance and supremacy."

Nathaniel Tilden of Tenterden, yeoman, wife Lydia, seven children, and seven servants. Certificates from Mr. Jno. Gee, Vicar of Tenterden,

---

* From the History of Sandwich, by William Boys, 4to, Canterbury, 1786-92.

26 Feb. 1634, Jno. Austin, Mayor of Tenterden, and Fregift Stace, jurat, 4 Mar. 1634.*

Jonas Austen, of Tenterden, Constance, his wife, and four children. Certificates from Mr. Jno. Gee, 1st Mar. 1634, Jno. Austin, Mayor, and Fregit Stace, jurat, 4 Mar. 1634.

Rob. Brook, of Maidstone, mercer, Ann, his wife, and seven children. Certificates from Samuel Marshall, mayor of Maidstone, Tho. Swinnok, jurat, Edw. Duke and Rob. Barrel, ministers, 14 Mar. 1634.

Tho. Heyward, of Aylesford, taylor, Susannah, his wife, and five children. Certificates from William Colepeper, Caleb Bancks, Edw. Duke, Han. Crispe, Franc. Froiden, cler. 14 Mar. 1634.

Will. Witherell, of Maidstone, schoolmaster, Mary, his wife, three children, and one servant. Certificates from Sam. Marshal, mayor of Maidstone, Tho. Swinnuck, Edw. Duke and Rob. Barrel, cl. 14 Mar. 1634.

Fannett . . . . of Ashford,† hemp dresser. Certificates from Edw. Chute, Edm. Hayes, vicar of Ashford, Elias Wood, parson of Hinxhill,‡ 4 Mar. 1634.

Tho. Boney and Han. Ewell, of Sandwich, shoemakers. Certificate from Mr. Tho. Warren, rector of St. Peters, in Sandwich, 14 Mar. 1634.

Will. Hatch, of Sandwich, merchant, Jane, his wife, five children and six servants. Certificate from Mr. Tho. Gardener, vicar of St. Mary's, Sandwich, 17 Mar. 1634.

Sam. Hinkley, of Tenterden, Sarah his wife, and four children. Certificates, Mr. Jno. Gee, vicar of Tenterden, Jn. Austin, mayor, Fregift Stace, jurat, 15 Mar. 1634.

Isaac Cole, of Sandwich, carpenter, Joan his wife, and two children. Certificate from Mr. Tho. Warren, rector of St. Peter, Sandwich, 14 Mar. 1634.

A servant. A certificate from Edm. Hayes, vicar of Ashford, 21 Mar. 1634.

Tho. Champion, of Ashford. Certificate from Edm. Hayes, vicar, 12 Mar. 1634.

---

* The year in this list must be understood 1634–5.

† In Kent, doubtless; though there were at that day no less than eight Ashfords.

‡ Hinksell, Hinxell. The same, in Kent.

Tho. Besbeech, of Sandwich, six children and three servants. Certificates from Tho. Warren, rector of St. Peter's, Sandwich, 13 Mar. 1634. Tho. Harman, vicar of Hedcorn, 6 Mar. 1634.

Jno. Lewis, of Tenterden, Sarah his wife and one child. Certificates from Jno. Gee, vicar of Tenterden, 20 Feb. 1634. Jno. Austin, mayor, and Fregift Stace, jurat, 1st Mar. 1634.

Parnel Harris, of Bow, London. Certificate from Jos. Leeth, vicar of Bow, London, 19 Mar. 1634.

James Sayers, of Northburn,* taylor. Certificate from Edw. Nicholls, vicar of Northburn, 2 Feb. 1634.

Comfort Starre, of Ashford, chirurgion. Three children and three servants. Certificates from Edm. Hayes, vicar of Ashford, 21 Mar. 1634. Jno. Honnywood, Tho. Godfrey, justices.

Jos. Rootes, of Great Chart. Cert. from Rob. Gorsham, curate of great Chart, 20 Mar. 1634.

Em. Mason, of Eastwell, wid. Certificate from Will. Sandford, rector of Eastwell, 16 Mar. 1634.

Margt. wife of Will Jones, late of Sandwich, now of New England, painter. Certificate from Tho. Gardiner, vicar of St. Mary's, Sandwich, 26 Mar. 1634.

Jno. Best, of St. George's, Canterbury, taylor. Certificate from Tho. Jackson, minister of St. Georges, Canterbury, ult. Feb. 1634.

Tho. Bridgen, of Faversham, husbandman, his . . . . . wife and two children. Certificates from Jno. Phillips, minister of Faversham, 5 March, 1634, Jno. Knowler, mayor, and Will. Thurston, jurat.

[In another part of the same work the following list is found, " of persons who have taken passage from the town and port of Sandwich for the American Plantations since the last certificate of such passengers returned into the office of Dover Castle." Whether their destination was for New England is left to conjecture. However, it is pretty certain that some of them found their way there eventually. The list is " certified under the seal of office of mayoralty, 9 June, 1637."]

Thomas Starr, of Canterbury, yeoman, Susan, his wife, and one child.

---

* In Kent, Northborne in some early topographies.

Edward Johnson, of Canterbury, joiner, Susan, his wife, seven children and three servants.

Nicholas Butler, of Eastwell, yeoman, Joice, his wife, three children and five servants.

Samuel Hall, of Canterbury, yeoman, Joan, his wife, and three servants.

Henry Bachelor, of Dovor, brewer, Martha, his wife, and four servants.

Joseph Bachelor, of Canterbury, taylor, Elizabeth, his wife, one child and three servants.

Henry Richardson, of Canterbury, carpenter, Mary, his wife, and five children.

Jarvis Boykett, of Charington, carpenter, and one servant.

John Bachelor, of Canterbury, taylor.

Nathaniel Ovell, of Dovor, cordwinder, and one servant.

Thomas Calle, of Faversham, husbandman, Bennett, his wife, and three children.

William Eaton, of Staple, husbandman, Martha, his wife, three children, and one servant.

Joseph Coleman, of Sandwich, shoemaker, Sara, his wife, and four children.

Matthew Smith, of Sandwich, cordwinder, Jane, his wife, and four children.

Marmaduke Peerce, of Sandwich, taylor, Mary, his wife, and one servant.

In the Historical Magazine some very valuable notes have been published, contributed by Hon. Henry C. Murphy, Minister at the Hague, being extracts from the city records at Leyden, and, by the kind permission of the publisher, Mr. C. B. Richardson, we now present such of the items as are interesting to the genealogist especially.*

1. JOHN ROBINSON, the minister. In 1622 his family consisted of himself, his wife Bridget, children James,† Bridget, Isaac, Mercy, Fear and

---

* This synopsis has been kindly furnished by Mr. W. H. Whitmore.

† Mr. G. Sumner reads this name *John*. See N. E. Hist. and Gen. Reg., xiii, 342.

Jacob, and a maid servant, Mary Hardy. In May, 1629, Bridget m. John Grynwich, student of theology, and Robinson's widow was a witness.

2. DEGORY PRIEST of London, m. Sarah Vincent, widow of John V. of London, Nov. 4, 1611. She m. 2d, in Leyden, 13 Nov. 1621, Goddard Godbert, and is there called "Sarah Allerton, widow of Degory Priest." (She was probably a relation of Isaac Allerton, and was married the same day.)

3. ISAAC ALLERTON, of London, m. 4 Nov. 1611, Mary Norris, of Newbury, Eng.

4. WILLIAM WHITE m. Feb. 1, 1612, Anna Fuller.

5. SAMUEL FULLER of London, (whose former wife was Elsie Glascock,) m. Agnes Carpenter of Wrentham,* Eng. William Hoyt was his brother-in-law, and Alice Carpenter was the bride's sister. Both were witnesses.

6. WILLIAM BRADFORD, of Austerfield, Eng., m. Nov. 30, 1613, Dorothy May of Witzbuts, Eng.

7. MOSES FLETCHER, (former wife was Maria Evans,) m. Sarah Dingby, widow of William D.

8. SAMUEL FULLER, (former wife was Anna Carpenter,) m. 27 May, 1617, Bridget Lee, whose mother Joos Lee was a witness.

9. EDWARD WINSLOW of London m. 16 May, 1618, Elizabeth Barker of Chetsum, Eng. Her niece, Jane Phesel, witnessed.

10. WILLIAM BASSETT, (former wife was Cecil Lecht,) m. Margaret Oldham, 13 Aug. 1611. He was published with Mary Butler, 19 March, 1611, but she died before marriage.

11. ROBERT CUSHMAN of Canterbury, Eng., (former wife Sarah Cushman,) m. 3 June, 1617, Mary Chingelton.

12. GEORGE MORTON, of York, Eng., m. 23 July, 1612, Julia Ann Carpenter. Her father Alexander C. and sister Alice C. were witnesses with Anna Robinson and Thomas Morton, brother of the groom.

13. JOHN JENNE of Norwich, Eng., m. 1 Nov. 1614, Sarah Carey of Moncksoon, Eng.

14. STEPHEN TRACY m. 2 Jan. 1621, Trifisa Le——.

15. RICHARD MASTERTON of Sandwich, Eng., m. Mary Goodall of Leicester, Eng., 26 Nov. 1619. His bro.-in-law John Ellis witnessed.

---

* Mr. Somerby does not find the Carpenter family at this early date in Wrentham, Eng. This name should probably be *Wrington*. See N. E. Hist. and Gen. Reg., xiv, 196.

Others, of the same congregation, were (16) WILLIAM PAUTES, who m. Wybra Hausen, 4 Dec. 1610; (17) RAYNULPH TICKENS, who m. 11 April, 1611, Jane White of Bebel; (18) WILLIAM BUCKRUM of Ipswich, Eng., who m. Elizabeth Neal of Scrooby, 17 Dec. 1611; (19) HENRY CRULLINGS, who m. 20 Dec. 1613, Dorothy Pettinger of Moortel; and (20) JOHN GILLIES of Essex, who had m. formerly Elizabeth Pettinger, and who m. Rosa Lylse of Yarmouth, 23 March, 1617.

Other names are:—
21. John Jennings of Colchester.
22. Edward Southworth.
23. William Buckrum of Ipswich. [See No. 18.]
24. Henry Cullens.
25. Edward Pickering of London.
26. Roger Wilkins.
27. Samuel Ferrier of Caen, France, [who m. 16 May, 1614, Mildreth Charles.]
28. Roger Chandler of Rochester.
29. Samuel Butler of Yarmouth.
30. Edmund Jepson.
31. Roger Wilson.
32. Henry Wilson of Yarmouth, who m. 16 May, 1616.
33. Zecheriah Berry.
34. John Spoonard.
35. Samuel Lee.
36. Stephen Butterworth.
37. Henry Jepson.
38. Roger Simons of Sarum.
39. Daniel Fairfield of Colchester.
40. Thomas Smith of Bury, [who m. Anna, dau. of John Crackston.]
41. John Codmore.
42. Thomas Hatfield.
43. Joseph Parsons of Colchester.
44. Robert Nelson.
45. Robert Warrener.
46. Raynulf Tickens, (brother-in-law of Robinson.)
47. Isaac Marcus.

48. Thomas Southworth.
49. Abraham Gray.
50. Henry Marshall.
51. Alexander Carpenter.
52. William Hoyt.
53. William Jepson.
54. Robert Smith.
55. John Keble.
56. Thomas Williams.
57. Jonathan Williams.
58. Henry Wood.
59. Israel Nes.
60. William Talbot.
61. John Ellis.
62. Anthony Clemens.
63. Roger White.
64. Anna Fuller.
65. Dillen Carpenter, (a female.)
66. Sarah Priest.
67. William Lysle.
68. John Reynolds of London.
69. Edward Goddar.
70. Catharine Carver.
71. William Talbot.
72. Elizabeth Neal.
73. Wybran Pautes, (a female.)
74. William Pautes of Norwich, (see No. 16.)
75. Joanna Lyons.
76. Pruce Jennings, (a female.)
77. Mary Finch.
78. William Brewer, a printer, and partner of Brewster, called also Thomas Brewer. A child of Brewster died 20 June, 1609.

It is to be hoped that these investigations will be continued, as the transcriber states he copied specially only those who came in the first four ships, and there is much more on the record. A letter from Robinson's church, April 28, 1625, announcing his death, is signed by Roger White.

[This work will now be found to contain complete lists of all the Emigrant Founders of New England, which have been brought to light. Those printed in the Register,—viz., in vol. i, pages 132, 377–9 ; vol. ii, page 407, and vol. ix, pages 265–8,—are here reprinted. Doubtless many of the Emigrants to Virginia, Barbadoes, and other Islands, found their way eventually to New England. All of these have been copied, and the most of them printed in the Register. Those which have not been printed will soon be.

I have thought it proper to append to the preceding List of Early Founders of New England, the King's Commission to Archbishop Laud, for governing that country. And notwithstanding its great importance in New England History, I am not aware that a perfect copy of it has ever been published in that country. Mr. Hubbard has, in his valuable History of New England, given an abstract of it, and Governor Pownall has given it in Latin in an Appendix to the Fourth Edition of his "Administration of the Colonies."

For similar reasons I give also the Commission to Sir Ferdinando Gorges, which constituted him Governor of New England. Both of these papers are copied from the originals, with the best care I can take for their accuracy.]

COMMISSION TO ARCHBISHOP LAUD, AND OTHERS, TO GOVERN NEW ENGLAND.

A Commission for y^e
makinge Lawes and Orders
for Government of English
Colonies planted in
Forraigne parts.
Dated xxviii° Aprilis
An° Caroli Regis x^{mo}
Anōq Dm̄. 1634.

Charles by the grace of God King of England Scotland ffrañce and Ireland Defender of the Faith &c.

To the most reverend Father in God our welbeloved and most faithfull Councellor, William, by divine Providence, Archb^{pp} of Canterburie, of all England primate, and Metropolitan, our welbeloved and most faithfull

Councello^r Thomas Lord Coventry, Lord Keeper of the greate Seale of England. The most reverend ffather in Christ, our welbèloved and faithfull Councello^r Richard by Divine Providence Archb^{pp} of Yorke Primate and Metropolitan, our welbeloved and most faithfull Cozens and Councellors, Richard Earle of Portland o^r high Trēr of England, Henry, Earle of Manchester, Lord Keeper of our privie Seale, Thomas Earle of Arundell and Surrey Earle Marshall of England, Edward Earle of Dorsett, Chamberlaine to o^r most deare Consort, the Queene And our welbeloved and faithfull Councello^r Fraunces Lord Cottington, Chauncello^r and Vnder Treasuro^r of o^r Exchequer, Sr Thomas Edmonds, knight, Treasuror of o^r Howshold, Sr Henry Fane knight, Comptroller of the same Howshold, Sr John Coke, knight, one of our prime Secretaries, and Sr Fraunces Windebancke, knight, one of our prime Secretaries Greeting Whereas

Very manie of our subiects and of our late Fathers of blessed memorie our Soueraigne Lord James King of England, by meanes of Lycence Royall, not onlie with desire of enlarging ye Territories of o^r Empire, but cheifely out of a pious and religious affection and desire of Propogatinge the Ghospell of our Lord and Saviour Jesus Christ, have Planted large Colonies of the English Nation in divers Partes of the world altogeather vnmanured and voyde of Inhabitants, or occupied of the barbaroas People that haue noe knowledge of Divine Wor^{pp} Wee being willing graciouslie to provide a remedie for the tranquillitie and quietnes of those People, and being very Confident of your faith Wisdome, Justice and provident Circumspection, haue Constituted yo^u the aforesaid Archb^{pp} of Canterbury Lord Keeper of the greate Seale of England, The Archb^{pp} of Yorke, The Lord Treasuro^r of England, Lord Keeper of the privie Seale, The Earle Marshall of England, Edward Earle of Dorsett, ffrauncis Lord Cottington, Sr Thomas Edmonds knight; Sr Henry Fane, knight, Sr John Coke, knight, and Sr Frauncis Windebancke, knight, or any five or more of yo^u o^r Commissioners. And to yo^u five or more of yo^u Wee doe giue and committ Power for the Gouernment and safetie of the said Colonies drawne, or wch out of the English Nation into those partes shalbe drawne, to make Lawes Constitutions and Ordinances p'tayning either to the publique state of those Colonies or the private proffit of them, and concerning the lands, Goods, Debts and Succession in those partes, and how they shall demeane themselves towards forraigne Princes and their People, or how they shall beare themselues towards vs and our Subiectes as well in any forraigne Partes whatsoever, or on yᵉ Seas in those partes or in their returne sayling home, or which may appertaine to yᵉ maintenance of the Clergie Government, or to the cure of Soules amonge the People living and exercising Trade in those partes by designing out congruent portions arising in Tithes oblations and other thinges there accordinge to your sound descretions in politicall and Civill Causes, and by having the aduise of twoe or three Bᵖᵖˢ for the setlinge, makeing and ordering of the busines for designing necessarie Ecclicall and Clergie Portions which yoʷ shall cause to be called and taken to yoᵘ, and to make Provision against the Violators of those Lawes Constitutions and Ordinances, by imposinge penalties and mulctes, imprisonmᵗ (if there be cause, and that the qualitie of the offence doe require it by deprivation of member or life to be inflicted) with power also, (our assent being had,) to remove, displace yᵉ Governor or Rulers of those Colonies for causes which to yoʷ shall seeme lawfull, and others in their stead to Constitute, and to require an Accompt of their Rule and Government, And whome yoʷ shall finde culpable, either by Deprivation from the Place or by Imposition of a mulct vpon the Goods of them in those Partes to be levied, or banishment from the Provinces in which they have been Governoʳˢ, or otherwise to Chastice according to the qualitie of the fault And to Constitute Judges and Magistrates politicall and Civell for Civill Causes and vnder the power and forme which to yoᵘ fiue or more of yoʷ with the Bpps Vicegereull (provided by the Archbᵖᵖ of Canterburie for the time being) shall seeme expedient And to ordayne Courtes Pretorian and Tribunall as well Ecclicall as Civell of Judgmente to determine of the forme and manner of proceeding in the same, And of appealing from them in matters and Causes as well Cryminall as Civill, Personall, reall and mixt, And to yᵉ Seates of Justice what may be equally and well ordered and what crymes, faultes, or excesses of Contractes, or iniuries ought to belonge to yᵉ Ecclicall Courte and Seate of Justice PROVIDED NEVERTHELESSE That the Lawes, Ordinances and Constitutions of this kind shall not be put in execution before oʳ Assent be had therevnto in writing vnder oʳ Signet, signed at least. And this Assent being had therevnto and the same publiquely proclaymed in yᵉ Provinces in which they are to be executed. Wee will and Command that those Lawes, Ordinances, and Constitutions more fully to obtayne strength and be confirmed shalbe inviolablie observed of all men whom they shall concerne NOTWITHSTANDING it shalbe lawfull for yoʷ five or more of yo^w as is aforesaid (although those Lawes Constitutions and ordinances shalbe proclaymed with our Royall Assent,) to change, revoke and abrogate them, and other new ones in forme aforesaid from time to time to frame and make as is aforesaid, and to new evills arisinge or daungers to applie new remedies as is fitting soe often as to yo^u shall seeme expedient.

Furthermore yo^u shall understand wee have Constituted yo^u or every fiue of yo^w the aforesaid Archb^{pp} of Canterbury, Thomas Lord Coventrie Lord Keeper of the Great Seale of England, Richard Archb^{pp} of Yorke, Richard Earle of Portland, Henry Earle of Manchester, Thomas Earle of Arundell and Surrey, Lord Cottington, Sr Tho: Edmondes, Knight, Sr Henry Fane, Knight, Sr John Coke, Knight, and Sr Fraunces Windebancke, Knight, o^r Commissioners to heare and determine according to yor sound discretions, all manner of Complaintes, either against those Colonies or the Rulers and Gouerno^{rs} at the instance of the parties greived, or at the Accusation brought from home or from thence, betweene them and their members to be moved, and to call ye Parties before yo^u, and to the Parties and their Procurators from hence or from thence being heard, the full complement of Justice to be exhibited. GIVING vnto yo^u, or any fiue or more of yo^w Power, that if yo^u shall finde any of the Colonies aforesaid, or any of the Cheife Rulers vpon the Iurisdiction of others by vniust Possession or Vsurpation, or one against another makeing greivance, or in Rebellion against vs, or withdrawing from our Allegeance, or o^r Mandate not obeying (consultation first with vs in that case had,) to cause those Colonies or the Rulers of them for the Causes aforesaid, either to returne to England, or to Comañd them to other places Designed, euen as according to your sound discretions it shall seeme to stand with equitie, Iustice and necessitie.

MOREOVER WEE DOE GIUE vnto yo^u or any fiue of yo^u Power and speciall Comãund over all the Charters and Letters Patentes, and Rescriptes Royall of the Regions, Provinces, Islandes or Lands in other Partes graunted raising Colonies to cause them to be brought before yo^w and the same being reviewed, if any surreptiously, or vnduely hath bine obtayned; or that by ye same Privilege, Liberties or Prerogatives hurtfull to vs or o^r Croune or to forraigne Princes haue bine preiudicially suffered and graunted, the same being better made knowne vnto yo^w fiue, or more of yo^w, to command them according to the Lawes and Customes of England to bee revoked, and to doe such other thinges which to y⁶ Government profitt and safeguard of the aforesaid Colonies and of oʳ Subiectes resident in the same shalbe necessarie.

AND THERFORE wee doe Commaund yoʷ that about the Premises, at Dayes and times which for thies thinges yoʷ shall make provision, that yoᵘ be diligent in attendance as it becometh yoʷ Giuing in Precept also, and firmely enioyning, Wee doe giue Comañd to all and singular Cheife Rulers of Provinces into which the Colonies aforesaid have bine drawne or shalbe drawne and concerning y⁶ Colonies themselves concerning others that haue any interest therein that they giue attendance vpon yoᵘ and be observant and obedient to yoʳ Warrantes in those Affaires as often as need shall require, and euen as in oʳ name.

IN TESTIMONIE WHEREOF wee haue caused these oʳ Lreˢ to be made Patentes. Witnesse Oʳ selfe at Westminster the 28ᵗʰ Day of Aprill in y⁶ 10ᵗʰ yeare of oʳ Raigne

By Writt from the Privy Seale

[*Endorsement.*] Willis

Commission for y⁶ making Lawes and Orders for Government of English Colonies planted in foreign parts. Dated 28ᵗʰ April 1634.

State Paper Office.

COMMISSION TO SIR FERDINANDO GORGES AS GOVERNOR OF NEW ENGLAND. BY THE KING.

Manyfesting Our Royall pleasure for the establishing a generall Govern'mt in Our Territorye of New England for prevention of those evills that otherwise might Ensue for default thereof—

Forasmuch as Wee haue vnderstood and been credibly informed of the many inconueniences and mischiefs that haue growne aud are like more and more to arise amongst Our Subjects allready planted in the parts of New England by reason of the severall opinions differing humors and many other differences springing up betweene them and daily like to encrease, and for that it rested not in the power of the Councill of New England (By our Gracious ffathers royall Charter established for those affaires) to redress the same, Without wee take the whole manageing thereof into Our owne hands, and apply therevnto Our immediate power and authority, Which being perceived by the principall undertakers of those businesses, They haue humbly resigned the said Charter unto us, that thereby there may bee a speedy order taken for reformation of the aforesaid Errors and mischeifs. And knowing it to bee a Duty proper to our Royall Justice not to suffer such Numbers of Our people to runne to ruine and so religious and good intents to languish for want of timely remedie and Soueraigne assistance Wee haue therefore graciously accepted of the said Resignation and doe approue of their good affections to a seruice soe acceptable to God and vs, And wee haue seriously aduised with Our Councill both of the way of Reformation and of a person meet and able for that imployment by whose grauity, moderation and experience Wee haue hopes to repair what is amiss and settlem^t of those affaires to the good of Our people and honour of Our Gouernm^t. And for that purpose Wee haue resolued with Our selfe to imploye Our Servant fferdinando Gorges knight, as well for that Our Gracious ffather of blessed memory as Wee haue had for a long time good experience of his fidelity, circumspection and knowledge of his Gouernem^t in martiall and civill affaires, besides his understanding of the State of those Countreys wherein he hath been an immediate mover and a principall Actor, to the great prejudice of his estate, long troubles and the loss of many of his good ffreinds and servants in making the first discovery of those Coasts, and taking the first seizure thereof as of right belongs to vs Our Crowne and dignity, and is still resolued according to Our Gracious pleasure to prosecute the same in his owne person, Which resolution and most comendable affection of his to serve vs therin, as We highly approve, Soe Wee hold it a property of Our princely care to second him with Our Royall and ample authority Such as shalbee meet for an employment soe eminent and the performance of Our Service therin, wherof Wee haue thought itt fitt to make publick Declaration of Our said pleasure, That therby it may appear to our good Subjects the resolution Wee haue graciously to prouide for the peace and future good of those whose affection leads them to any such vndertaking, and withall to Signifye that Our further will and pleasure is, That none bee permitted to goe into any those parts to plant or inhabitt. But that they first acquaint Our said Gouerno^r therwith, or such other as shalbee deputed for that purpose during his aboad heer in England, And who are to recciue from him or them allowance to pass with his or their further directions where to sitt downe most for their perticuler commoditycs and publick good of our Service (Sauing and reseruing to all those that haue Joyned in the Surrender of the Great Charter of New England and haue Grants immediately to bee holden of us for their Severall plantations in the said Countrye, ffree liberty at all times hereafter to go themselues and also to send such Numbers of people to their plantacoñs as by themselues shall bee thought conuenient Heerby strictly charging and commanding all our Officers and others to whom it shall or may appertaine, to take notice of this our pleasure and to be careful the same bee firmely obserued as they or any of them shall answer the same at their vttermost perill. Giuen at the Court of Whitehall the 23. day of July 1637. and in the Thirteenth yeare of Our Raigne.

State Paper Office.

SIR FERDINANDO GORGES, KT.

The man who persevered so long, and against such adverse fortune, to colonize New England, has scarcely received from the historian notice proportionate to his sacrifices. Nor is it proposed here to do more than to bring into view a few additional materials for the biographer of Sir Ferdinando Gorges. It is a very common and it may be said perhaps a very natural error, for biographers to claim too much for their heroes. It has been recently asserted* that Sir Ferdinando was "the father of English colonization in America." We know of no process of reasoning by which to arrive at that conclusion. And according to some notions which have crept into our mind, we feel quite sure that, instead of calling Sir Ferdinando the father of colonization, we should call him at least the greatgrandson of *that gentleman*. But we must waive discussion on that head, at present, as we are now to deal only with original papers.

The following pedigrees, from Heralds' Visitations in the British Museum, furnish the pedigree of Sir Ferdinando, and his relationship to others of the name. Lord Edward Gorges, it appears, was a first cousin to Edward Gorges, father of Sir Ferdinando. Robert Gorges, the son of Sir Ferdinando, had a commission as governor of New England, came here in 1623 with a colony, and settled at Weymouth; but returned in the course of the year. John, the other son, was father of Ferdinando Gorges, who published, in 1658, "America painted to the Life."

---

* See Historical Magazine, vol. iii, 336.

96   THE FOUNDERS OF NEW ENGLAND.

PEDIGREE OF GORGES.

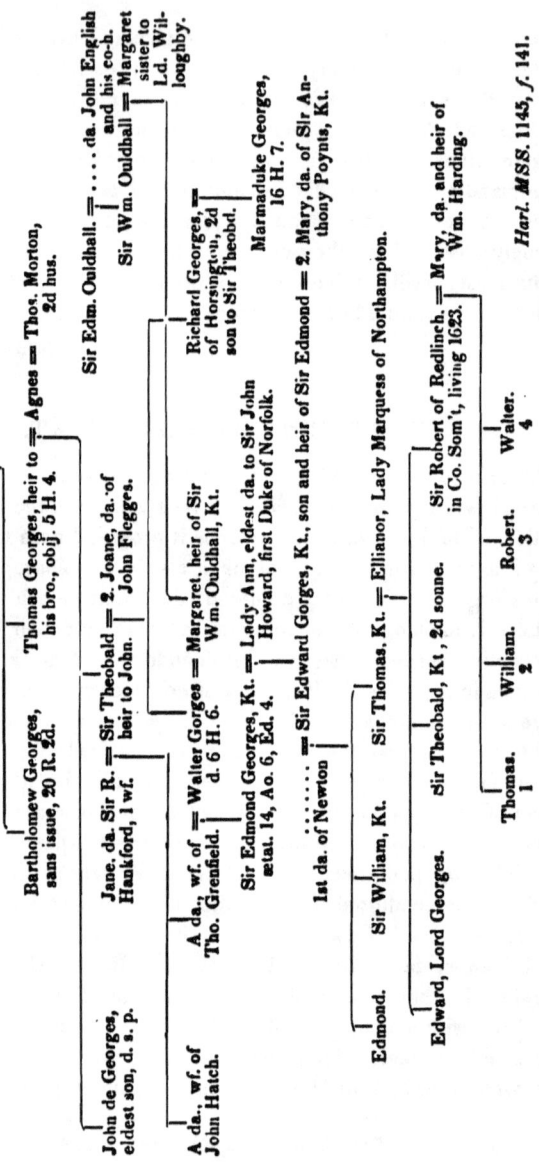

Ralphe de Georges lived 35 of Hen. 3. He had a son Sr. Ralphe, who had a wife Margaret.... This Sr. Ralphe de Gorges, Kt. was a wit. to the King's Charter for lands given to the Count of Atbridge, Anno 13 Ed. 1. Thomas, son of this Sr. Ralphe, by Inquisition 33 Ed. 1. His son, Ralphe de Georges, in the time of Ed. 2d. m. Ellianor, and had a da. Ellianor his co-heir, who m. Sr. Theobald Russell, Kt, proved by Inq. 15 Ed. 3. They had Randall Russell, and Theobald de Georges, see surnamed from his mother, ob. 4 Ric. 2.*

Bartholomew Georges, sans issue, 20 R. 2d.

Thomas Georges, heir to his bro., obij. 5 H. 4. = Agnes = Thos. Morton, 2d hus.

Sir Edm. Ouldhall. = ... da. John English and his co-h.

Sir Wm. Ouldhall = Margaret sister to Ld. Willoughby.

John de Georges, eldest son, d. s. p.

Jane, da. Sir R. Hankford, 1 wf. = Sir Theobald, heir to John.

= 2. Joane, da. of John Fleggs.

A da., wf. of John Hatch.

A da., wf. of Tho. Grenfield. = Walter Gorges, d. 6 H. 6.

Margaret, heir of Sir Wm. Ouldhall, Kt.

Richard Georges, of Horsington, 2d son to Sir Theobd.

Marmaduke Georges, 16 H. 7.

Sir Edmond Georges, Kt. ætat. 14, A⁰. 6, Ed. 4.

Lady Ann, eldest da. to Sir John Howard, first Duke of Norfolk.

.... = Sir Edward Gorges, Kt., son and heir of Sir Edmond = 2. Mary, da. of Sir Anthony Poynts, Kt.

1st da. of Newton

Edmond.

Sir William, Kt.

Sir Thomas, Kt. = Ellianor, Lady Marques of Northampton.

Edward, Lord Georges.

Sir Theobald, Kt, 2d sonne.

Sir Robert of Redlinch, in Co. Som't, living 1623. = Mary, da. and heir of Wm. Harding.

Thomas. 1 William. 2 Robert. 3 Walter. 4

Harl. MSS. 1145, f. 141.

* This Theobald De Russell, surnamed De Gorges, had a controversie concerninge his Armes adjudged in the King's Haste at the Siege before Callis, by Hen. Earle of Lane: Derby & Leicester Lo Seneschall of England & William De Clynton, Earle of Lincolne, Reignold De Cobham & Walter of many Bannerettes & Willm Lovell & Stephen Cosengton Kts Commissioners and Judges by Letters from the King of Englande & of France, for matters of Armes, &c.

THE FOUNDERS OF NEW ENGLAND.

Pedigree of Gorges (continued)

Sir Theobald Gorge, Kt. and Bart., 2 brother to John George, sonnes of Tho. Gorge,* sonne of Ralph

Walter Gorge = ... dau. and heire of Owld hale.

Sir Edm. Gorge, ward to Jo: Lo: Howard in the time of Edward 4th. = Ann, d. of the said John Lord Howard, Duke of Norfolk.

William Gorge. ..... da. of Sir .... Poynes. = Sir Edmond, Kt. = da. of Sir Jo. Newton, Kt., 2 wf.

Edmond Georg = ... da. of Sir John Walsh in Co. Glou.   Alice.   Margt.

Sir Thomas, Kt.   A dau. m. Incolus Gorge.   Sir Wm.   Robert.   Edward = Cicely, d. of Hyones of Wc.

Sir Ferdinando Gorge, Kt., 2d sonne. = ... da. Sir George Speake, Kt. of the Bath.

Sir Edward Gorge, Kt., living ao. 1623. =

Robert.   John.   Anne vx Ed. Tynt.   Dorothy vx.   Francis vx 1 Lutterell, 2 Sir Edward Southcott.   William 2. Thomas 3. Samuell 4.   Sir Robert of Wraxall, living 1623. = Mary. d. Sir Marmaduke Dayrell.   Dorothy vx Cary of Clovelly.   Elizabeth vx Trenchard of Wilts.

[*Harl. MSS.* 1445, f. 106.]

Sir William George of Wraxall, Kt. =

Robert George of Batcombe in Co. Somersett, 2d son, = Ann, da. of .... Webb of Batcombe.

Edward, 2d son.   Mary, wife to John Moore.   Henry of Batcombe, now living. = Barbara, da. of Tho. Baynard of Cullorne, in Co. Wilts.   Margaret, wf. to Edward Kinnersley.   1   Ann, wf. to John Guye.   2   John, 2.   Joyce, wf. to James Spencer.   3   Ann.   Christian, wf. to Tho. Stephens.   4

Thomas, son and heire, ætat. 5, annores, 1623.

[*Harl. MSS.* 1141, 73 b.

Signed   HE: GORGS.

---

* Several generations are omitted here, if the preceding pedigree is correct. According to that pedigree this Thomas Gorges was the 3d gen. from one Ralph de Gorges and the 7th gen. from the earliest mentioned Ralph. Burke's "Extinct and Dormant Baronetcies," (1844) p. 221, has a pedigree of this family, which, except omitting Thomas, grandson of the first Ralph, agrees with Pedigree No. 1, in these early generations. There are discrepancies, however, in later ones.

Sir Arthur Gorges, Chelsea, knighted 1597, d. 1625. He built a house on this site [of Stanley House] for his own residence. As the Queen [Eliz.] passd by the faire new building, Sir Arthur Gorges presented her with a faire jewell. *Sidney papers*—Letter from Rowland White to Sir Robert Sidney, 15 Nov. 1599. Sir Arthur was the intimate friend of Spencer, who made a beautiful elegy on the first Lady Gorges, dau. of Viscount Bindon, who d. 1590, entitled *Daphnaida*, and her husband is meant by Alcyon. Sir Arthur's second wife was the Lady Elizabeth, dau. of Henry, Earl of Lincoln, by which marriage he became possessed of Sir Thomas More's house, which, in 1619, he conveyed to Lionel, Lord Cranfield. He left by his second wife six children, viz., Arthur,(1) first son and heir, a. then 24 (1625), Timoleon,(2) Egremont, (3) Carew,(4) Henry,(5) Elizabeth.—*Faulkner's Hist. Chelsea*, i. 56–7, 2 *vols*. 8°. 1829.

On the south side of the church at Chelsea—

> Here sleeps, and feels no presure of this stone,
> He that had all the Gorges Souls in one, &c.

The generous and worthy gentleman Arthur Gorges, Esq., eldest son of Sir Arthur Gorges, Kt. The last surviving Branch of the first Male Line of that Honourable Family.—*Strype's Stow*, ii. B. vi. p. 72.

In the chancel of the church of St. Michael near Exeter, parish of Hevitree, is this inscription to " Thomas Gorges of Hevitree, Esq., and Rose, his wife. He departed this life the 17th of October, 1670; and she the 14th day of April, 1671.

> The lovinge Turtell havinge mist her mate
> Beg'd she might enter ere they shut the gate
> Their dust lies whose soules to Heaven are gonne
> And waite till Angells rowle away the stone.
>
> *Jenkins's Hist. Exeter*, 441.

Arms.—Gorges of Somersetshire bear—Argent a whirlpool azure. Crest—A greyhound's head erased argent collared gules.

A Devonshire branch bore—Ermin a fesse between three fleurs-de-lis gules. Another—Ermin a fesse between three roses gules. Crest—An annulet, stoned azure. See Burke's *Heroldic Dictionary*.

EMIGRANTS FOR ST. CHRISTOPHERS, &c.

[The following Lists from the same volume as the preceding were copied and furnished to the Register by Mr. H. G. SOMERBY.]

Register of the names
of all ye Passinger w^{ch}
Passed from ye Porte of
London for on whole
yeare Endinge at
Xp'^{mas} 1635

---

vi Januarii 1634

Theis under written names are to be transported to St. Christophers and the Barbadoes, James Romsey M^r bound thither have taken ye oath of Allegeance.

Name	Age	Name	Age	Name	Age
John Phillips	21	Willm Burt	22	Edward Jones	21
John Allin	23	John Bowes	23	Mark Ellvyn	20
Davie Johnes	24	Henry Cappledike	20	Henry Purslym	18
Wm White	30	Robt. Stratford	16	Richard Chitting	23
Humfrey Davies	22	Robert Holland	19	Tho: Marfutt	22
Wm Camion	21	Tho: Borne	22	Richard Edmonds	18
Edward Lampeugh	35	Edward Roberts	25	Wm Prichard	25
George Cliffe	26	John Carter	26	Tho: Arnold	18
Abram Jn°son	27	George Sutton	19	Richard Chamblis	19
Henrie Wells	23	Edward Jennor	24	Edward Brunt	25
John Usher	26	Joseph Glade	20	George Stokes	23
Edmond Knight	21	Peter Monk	29	Henry Fookes	21
Tho: Rasbottom	23	Richard Coke	38	Robert Granger	21
Wm Griggson	14	Isack Peter	20	Wm Walter	26
Richard Jones	23	Phillipp Squier	20	John Rods	20
Michell White	18	Bartholomew Flade	24	Ezechell Clements	20
Richard Borne	24	Richard Lawrence	20	Tho: Carpenter	20
Edward Fletcher	20	Daniell Smith	20	Tho: Smith	17
Francis Sowthe	19	John Symes	17	John White	27
John Conny	20	Robert Kett	22	John Watkinson	22
Robert Skarvill	21	Suzan Hudson	20	Joseph Pardy	23
Edward Robinson	18	Mary Sea	16	Robert Langredge	23
John Holland	15	John Shettleworth	28	Jn° Etherington	17
Edward Ash	20	Richard Fryme	26	George White	27
Tho. Sandby	17	Robt Holme	22	Tho: Cockey	25
Tho. Greene	24	John More	28	Ant° Blackgrove	24
Mark Theody	18	Richard Pence	45	John Higgins	20

Willm Hodgson	20	Robt. Ground	22	Robert Gilby	18
Tho: Jenkynns	23	William Bruton	22	Robert Baker	50
Jnº Greenewood	26	William Walton	22	Tho: Peck	20
John Place	22	Willm Seward	26	Willm Harris	35
Wm Hayman	36	Henry Rymes	40	John Towne	27
Edward Savage	20	Henry Iles	17	Christian Mynnikyn	19
Jo: Conniers	21	Bryan Erle	21		
John Moore	30	John Fox	19		

17 Februarij 1634

Theis under written names are to be transported to the Barbadoes imbarqued in yͤ Hopewell Capten Tho: Wood Mʳ bound thither. The passengers have taken the oath of Allegeance and Supremacie.

Willm Usher	22	John Faux	36	Tho: Letteny	20
Rich. Hanby	23	Joseph Bryan	20	Robert Porter	20
Richard Jackson	17	Nevill Hutchins	20	John Hughes	20
Joh. Hill	19	Wm Walters	22	Henry Akyns	22
Richard Clynton	23	Willm Puttex	20	Robert Rember	21
Jnº Harrison	46	Archibald Weyer	18	Robert Mills	19
James Read	19	Nathaniell Cobham	17	John Davies	25
Dunston Rember	20	Jarvice Dodderidge	21	Thomas Crowder	21
Wm Owen	23	John Derborn	22	Richard Purnell	21
Jnº Free	25	Willm Seriff	19	Robert Lynley	20
Richard Gane	19	John Offword	24	Henry Holmes	44
Thomas Richards	19	Tho: Lee	20	John Key	30
John Nicks	23	Robert Richards	18	John Williams	21
Martin Perkynn	20	George Hiter	18	John Fowler	24
Antº Blades	24	John Dreadd	17	John Owen	20
Robert Dymond	29	Arthur Wynd	17	Owen Williams	21
Tho: Dayes	20	Richard Osborn	22	Tho: Drew	26
Wm Walker	21	John Phillipps	37	Wm Bunystedd	21
Ralph Harwood	23	John Steevens	13	Edward Jnºson	20
Phillipp Philpott	30	John Reddhedd	28	John Bownd	20
James Pallister	28	Wm Gibson	18	John Haies	30
Richard Clark	21	Tho: Waterman	27	John Lyon	18
Daniell Baker	20	Tho: Jones	19	Willm Corfer	24
John Tayler	23	Jo: Nisom	23	Thomas Trigg	21
Thomas Prosser	20	Edward Layton	30	Robert Nisbett	19
John Eaton	20	Wm Benson	28	Willm Caddy	21
Tho: Smith	21	John Whitehedd	23	John Cassedy	20
John Johnson	18	Richard Barnard	23	Alexander More	24
Richard Holmes	24	Henry Long	21	Richard Wellyn	25
Ralph Terrett	24	John Wilks	22	Richard Griffs	24
Henry Tatnum	20	Tho: Wellman	21	Arthur Yeomans	24
Alexander Smith	18	Tho: Gaton	25	Nicholas Hobson	23
John Crapp	37	Wm Allin	25	Wm Marrow	25

EMIGRANTS FOR ST. CHRISTOPHERS, &C.

Francis Dene	21	Phillipp Cartwrite	20	Wm Seere	22
John Philpott	16	John Loftis	21	Wm Levyns	22
John Strattergood	18	Michell Rocks	21	Jo: Hamond	17
Wm Cant	19	Jo: Ling	45	Edward Pullin	27
Henrie Speckman	27	Tho: Sherman	26	James Cullimor	22
John Yats	19	Wm Jackson	30	Jo: Depark	28
Wm Ranse	27	James Goldingham	32	Richard Walton	21
George Selman	16	Rich. Rainolds	19	Robert Collie	20
Nicholas Blades	21	Jo: Nokes	20	Joseph Hepworth	33
John Clark	24	Francs Symonds	21	Willm Walters	32
Tho: Everie	19	Thomas Lurtray	21	Daniell Smith	33
Tho: Medwell	31	James Anderson	19	Richard Trueman	24
Jo: Basher	20	Walter Jago	20	Wm Masters	21
James Ellerton	18	John Bead	22	Jo: Clere	26
Richard Hands	19	John Young	19	Randall Ogden	19
Medusala Watts	20	Tho: Hubbard	20	Tho: Browne	21
Tho: Hames	19	Edward Browne	24		

26 Martij 1635.

This under written name is to be imbarqued in the Peter Bonaventure Tho: Harman Mr bound for ye Barbadoes and St Christophers p' Certificate from St Andrewes p'rish Holborne: And attestacon from Justice Grimston, and Justice Sheppard hath taken the oaths of Allegeance & Supremacie.   William Banks 21 yeeres

To be Imbarqued In the Peter Bonavtr de Lond Capt. Harman Vsª Barbades. Theis p'ties here under expressed have brought Certeficat from two Justices of peace that the toke the oathe of Allegª & S'ppremacie and Also cert frō ye ministr of the p'ishe the 3d Aprill 1635.

Tho: Hathorne aged 22 yers	Jane Maddockes 21	Margrett Ellgate	24
Wm Morrison 23	Alce Mare 22	Margrett Hartforde	22
Ralph Vaughan 22 & ½			

4th Aprill 1635

In the Peter Bonavtr de Lond Capt Harman for Barbades. Theis two p'ties brought Cert from two Justices of peace and the ministr of their Conformity accord' to order.

Wm Clerke   29 yers. | Tho: Sergeant   23 yers.

EMIGRANTS FOR ST. CHRISTOPHERS, &C.

3 Aprilis 1635. At Gravesend.

Theis under written names are to be transported to St. Christophers imbarqued in the Paul of London, Jo. Acklin, M[r] bound thither, there was Cert: brought from the Minister of St. Catherins of their conformitie of their discipline and orders to y[e] Church of England the men did take y[e] oath of Alleg. and Supremacie.

Ralph Reason	yeres 23	W[m] Scarsbrick	23	Edward Gray	32
Edward Merrifield	19	W[m] Church	21	Jo: Watts	21
Robert Wade	35	John Reinolds	23	Edward Fisher	27
Will[m] Haies	24	Henry Bagin	22	Ric[h] Crowder	28
Geo: Rishford	24	W[m] Lamyn	21	Ric[h] Preston	21
Mathew Moyses	17	Hanna Roper	23	Ric[h] Older	24
Robert Richardson	20	Henry Lee	30	W[m] King	18
Jo: Mountain	20	Edward Smallman	21	Jo: Holmes	22
Jo: Willis	29	Robert Atkinson	23	Nic[o] Sedden	20
Jo: French	18	Tho: Fearfax	22	Fra: Stott	32
Tho: Watson	29	Mathew Turner	46	Phillipp Jeflings	25
David Evans	22	Edward Gass	20	Robert Spurr	24
Steeven Garret	19	Henry Sentence	20	Tho: Spendergrass	24
W[m] Beddle	19	Edmond Davies	21	Nic[o] Hollis	20
Richard Lock	20	Edward Barnes	16	Ric[h] Danes	20
Abram Watson	19	Tho: Nott	18		
James Carter	25	Jo: Adams	16		

In the Peter Bonaventure, Tho: Harman M[r] bound for the Barbadoes theis under written names p' order: they have taken y[e] oaths of Supremacie and Allegeance.

Tho: Berkynn	yeres 24	W[m] Weston	16	James Robards	20
Jo: Westgarth	28	W[m] Houseman	12	Ric[h] Clark	19
Jo: Sweeting	26	Ric[h] Chapman	40	Geo: Plankett	19
James Townson	29	Tho: Cutler	35	W[m] Marrowdin	19
Ric[h] Dawson	28	James Jackson	33	Jo: Alliday	20
Tho: Greenwood	15	Jo: Smitheman	23	Walter Gibson	25
Tho: Iveson	36	Robert Savage	21	Jo: Wynkles	20
Tho: Hywood	22	Geo: Penny	24	Jo: Vynn	17
W[m] Banks	23	Jo: Pattman	23	Robert Roe	19
Jo: Greealy	20	Tho: Coke	30	Maurice Williams	18
Daniell Davies	26	Jo: Symonds	19	Dennis Mortagh	30
Robert Braban	29	Jo: Boone	12	Jo: Dukkarth	31
Jo: Thomas	25	Nic[o] Evans	16	Ric[h] Mansfield	22
Ric[h] Leech	22	Jo: Mydhouse	15	Gregorie Ogell	15
Ric[h] Abbott	20	Ric[h] Hollinby	20	W[m] Whitlock	31
Ambrose Huett	27	W[m] Lodge	13	Jo: Long	20
Jo: White	25	Isack Pratt	22	Jo: Thompson	31
Jo: Weston	26	Jo: Evans	17	Tho: Farmer	22

Rich Brownley	19	Capten Jacob Lake	30	Tho: Lamberd	23
Mathew Westwood	18	Luke Stokes	35	Geo: Chapman	17
Jo: Mather	21	Richard Speed	35	Wm Aston	17
Robert Pendred	40	Phillipp Henson	21	Adrian Coke	27
David Robinson	20	Arthur Watkyns	25	Robert Philkyn	25
Willm Beckkitt	26	Jo: Joyner	25	Jno Sympson	29
Tho: Evans	20	Jo: Dent	30	Steeven Greenly	16
Jo: Hynd	24	Robert Jnoson	26	Mary Loveley	35
Wm Mecham	20	Jo: Sawcott	18	Ann Loveley	10
Roger Wills*	20	Jo: Bunce	18	Margaret Lucocks	27
Tho: Tedder	19	Jo: Robinson	26	Annis Percy	24
Jo: Sessions	22	Rich Pell	22		
Daniell Dennis	22	Jo: Disherd	22		

xiiijo Aprilis 1635

Theis under written names are to be transported to the Barbadoes imbarqued in the Faulcon de London. Tho: Irish Mr p' Certificate from the Minister of the p'ish of their conformity to the orders of the church of England. The men have taken the oaths of Allegeance and Supremacie.

Gabriell Bolt	29	Jo: Belton	48	John Scott	16
Owen Bliss	30	Nicolas Flitcroft	16	Robert Jones	25
Geo: Say	26	Wm Bingham	18	Nathaniell Write	32
Bassell Terry	22	Humfrey Morris	18	John Jones	24
Marmaduke Turner	21	Jo: Dallinger	16	Tho: Wallis	27
Jo: Bassett	19	Jo: Rogers	34	Toby Hazell	20
Jo: Sheering	26	Jo: Spyer	32	Geo: Clark	15
Henrie Biddleston	17	Francis Smith	20	Tho: Roberts	18
Tho: Lett	22	Abraham Halloway	20	Marmaduke Crosby	28
Samvel Stor [or Ston, or Stow]	17	Joseph Drap'	21	Geo: Harris	17
		Tho: Bromby	59	Roger Sawter	17
James Burt	13	Jo: Bromby	27	Marie Perry	18
Charles Fall	19	Jesper Giggon	18	Elizabeth Elson	18
Wm Sennott	20	John Brumwell	22	Bridget Gerden	19
Jo: Browne	20	Rich Dent	17	Katherin Hill	20
Tho: Webb	18	Thomas Gualmay	22	Marie Newcom	17
Jo: Hopwood	20	Richard Snathe	19	Benedicte Sherhack	20
Nico Wade	19	Richard Cockman	20	Marie Crew	19
Robert Davers	14	Thomas Allin	22	Elizabeth Long	21
Henry Dye	20	Valentine Love	18	Winifred Hand	20
Edward Bull	22	Robert Hapley	21	Elizabeth Curtis	22
Farford Goldsmith	22	Tho: Metcalf	20	Wm Sturgis	18
Tho: Crispin	19	Wm Knight	30	Tho: Knowles	16
Francis Sheeres	26	Henrie Gilder	18	Peter Lostell	14
John Bathe	23	George Lee	16	Walter Holburd	24
Smith Baker	28	Anto Goldsworth	18		
James Hibbins	17	John Church	21		

16 Aprilis 1635.

Theis p'ties hereafter expressed are to be transported to the Island of Providence imbarqued in ye Expectacion Cornelius Billinge M^r, having taken the oaths of Allegeance and Supremacie: As likewise being conformable to the Church of England; whereof they brought testimonie from the Ministers and Justices of Peace, of their Abodes.

Francis Smith	36	Edward Horsham	14	Katherin Webb	22
Tho: Palmer	18	Richard Trendall	16	Elizabeth Scott	20
Leonard Smith	22	Wm Read	16	Marie Howes	18
Mathew Hamblen	38	Mathew Pippin	20	Dorothy Lawrence	28
Wm Lynlie	58	Mary Baker	42	Elizab: Horsham	16
Christian Whetston	19	Elisha Bridges	16	Alice Goldham	26
Wm Cawdle	19	Willm̄ Thorp	30	Richard Price	14
Florence Dickenson	19	Elizabeth Thorp	20	Richard Lane	38
Jo: Baker	42	Elizabeth Thorp	2	Alice Lane	30
Jo: Martin	30	Joan Felver	50	Samvell Lane	7
Wm Smith	20	Margaret Rollright	45	Jo: Lane	4
Ant^o Dowsell	20	Ellin Cooper	24	Oziell Lane	3
Richard Slie	20	Elizabeth Coke	20	Jo: Atkinson	36
Francis Dales	20	Marie Chaddock	20	Love Atkinson	38
Peter Ambrey	32	Elizabeth Hamond	25	Elizabeth Owen	30
Tho: Feld	18	Alice Awbrey	29	Marie Milward	21
Edward Hassard	24	Elizabeth Lawrence	26	Isack Barton	27
Richard Bull	17	Ann Noble	21	Abram Ray	20
Richard Reinolds	16	Marie Harrowigg	21	Dorcas Horsham	40
Wm Crakins	15	Millicent Leech	28	Marie Griffin	17
Jo: Totnell	16	Marie Goodwyn	20		

24 Aprilis 1635.

Theis under written names are to be transported to the Island of Providence imbarqued in the Expectacion aforesaid, the p'ties have taken ye oath of Alleg^e:

Nicholas Riskym̄er	31	Jo: Bloxsall	28	Jo: Saracele	17
Wm Randall	26	Sam: Gooden^{n}ff	22	Tho: Wilson	18
Andrew Leay	24	Edward Hastings	23		
Jo: Leay	25	Tho: Hobbs	18		

Theis under written names are to be transported to the Barbadoes and St. Christophers, imbarqued in the Ann & Elizabeth Jo: Brookehaven, Capten and M^r having taken the oaths of Allegeance and Supremacie. As

EMIGRANTS FOR ST. CHRISTOPHERS, &C.

also being conformable to the orders and discipline of the Church of England and no Subsedy Men, whereof they brought test from the Minister of St. Katherins neere yᵉ Tower of London

John Crofts	30	Willm Harris	23			
Jo: Mason	20	John Turpin	22	**WOMEN.**		
Jo: Oram	21	Francis Saidwell	18	Katherin Lloyd	19
Christopher Fish	24	Mathew Rogers	21	Suzan Greene	20
Owen Androwe	18	Bryan Bourk	19	Margerie Barran	19
Robert Anderson	22	Antᵒ Taylor	26	Elizabeth Benñing	18
John Greene	25	Andrew Carr	23	Elizabeth Bruster	18
Joseph Wallington	19	Owen Garret	20	Joan Smith	27
John Haieward	22	John Frazill	29	Suzan More	21
Thomas Martin	16	John Porter	24	Alice Dixon	21
Edmond Holloway	17	Charles Pollington	26	Jane Stafford	29
Thomas Pierce	19	Charles Jackson	18	Alice Hilton	18
William Hayward	18	Edward Bacon	25	Katherin Russell	20
Edward Wilkinson	17	Thomas Robinson	31	Mary Powell	23
Richard Gale	16	Patrick Conly	21	Debora Winke	21
Robert Tratt	21	George Goddin	31	Rebeca Bedding	18
Thomas Redman	16	Arthur Roker	20	Mathew Page	20
Willm Grubb	16	Tho: Dale	28	Ann Spicer	26
John Golding	21	John Davies	19	Mary Jones	20
Clement Hutchinson	20	Tho: Burton	19	Margery Harding	20
Bartholomew Bennet	18	Hugh Wynstonly	20	Marie Kinderslie	26
Thomas Tyler	21	Bartholomew Draper	20		
John Prichard	20	Robert Brook	25	Nicholas Greene	18
Giles Barnes	19	Hugh Tawyer	18	Robert Laycock	18
Hugh Sadler	20	Wm Greene	17	Michell Estplynn	18
Harford Young	20	Patrick Connyer	20	James Bell	19
John Williams	16	Richard King	23	Frend Picto	20
Andrew Evans	16	Willm Barnes	17	John Whithedd	22
John Barret	16	Willm Taylor	23	Jo: Mallion	21
Joseph Walker	18	Robert Sennod	23	Tho: Bedlam	24
James Tate	17	Thomas Perkynn	29	Tho: Lone	19
John Smith	14	Willm Longwith	26	Thomas Wazell	21
Nathaniel Bolton	19	Tho: Gullifer	28	Edward Garrard	26
Wm Laydon	17	John Davies	18	John Coke	22
Thomas Avery	18	Richard Cawood	25	Jeremy Hartley	30
Tho: Leake	18	Richard Dynley	19	Gilbert Holdsworth	30
Davie Williams	17	Dennis Peke	20		

2ᵒ Maij 1635.

Theis under written names are to be transported to yᵉ Barbadoes imbarqued in the Alexander Capt. Burche and Gilbert Grimes Mʳ pʳ

EMIGRANTS FOR ST. CHRISTOPHERS, &C.

Certificate from the Minister where they late dwelt the men tooke the oaths of Alleg and Supremacie die et A° pred.

Name	yeres	Name		Name	
Willm Rapan	29	Jo: Phillipps	20	Rowland Plunkett	18
Leonard Staples	22	Richard Cribb	19	Teague Nacton	28
Jo: Stanford	24	Tho: Browne	18	Dermond O'Bryan	20
James Manzer	27	Jo: Greenwich	21	Charles Galloway	19
Jo: Watts	25	Jo: Nedson	19	James Montgomery	19
Tho: Clark	26	Edward Church	18	Jn° McCoury	28
Michell King	27	Ant° Threlcatt	19	Samvell Priday	20
Henry Broughton	20	Wm Willis	17	Samvell Farron	30
Geo: Ventimer	20	Clement Hawkins	16	Edmond Montgomery	26
Robert Hardy	18	Lewes Hughes	19	Olliver Bassett	14
Tho: Dabb	25	John Greene	22	Parry Wy	15
Geo: Norton	22	Richard Marshall	36	Daniell Burche	14
Wm Huckle	20	Mathew Calland	16	Richard Stone	13
Edward Kemp	29	Lewes David	28	Thomas Tayler	27
Wm Powell	19	Geo: White	18	Edmond Nash	21
Ralph Promd	26	Geo: Rudglie	17	Jo: Herring	28
Jo: Bullman	40	Dennis Mc Brian	18	Wm Beaton	24
Jo: Watts	19	Jo: Bussell	36	Tho: Roe	22
Wm Dench	16	James Driver	27	Edward Banks	35
Francis Peck	22	Hugh Johnes	22	Tho: Fludd	21
Jo: Benstedd	24	Tho: Gildingwater	30	David Collingworth	22
Symon Parler	24	John Ashurst	24	Wm Mathews	30
Richard Howseman	19	James Parkinson	23	Tymothie Goodman	27
Walter Jones	20	Willm Young	21	Tho: Penson	20
Phelix Lyne	25	Wm Smith	18	Wm Anderson	36
Arthur Write	21	Morgan Jones	31	Geo. Merriman	41
Lewes Willms	21	Jo: Richard	30	Jo: Dellahay	27
Wm Pott	18	Peter Flaming	16	Robert Lee	33
Thomas Gilson	21	Miles Farring	24	Jo: Jackson	24
Nic° Watson	26	Robert Atkins	23	Alexander de la Garde	27
Olliver Hookham	32	Beniamin Mason	23	Francis Marshall	26
Chri: Buckland	25	Tho: Rutter	22	Walter Lutterell	20
Jo: Hill	23	Jo: Howse	41	Jo: White	15
Anthony Skooler	20	Jo: Cole	20	Jo: Burton	17
Jo: Anderson	21	James Watts	35	Symon Wood	14
Wm Phillipps	17	Wm Crome	17	Robert Mussell	14
Jo: Befford	18	Phillipp Lovell	34	Richard Fane	15
Henry Yatman	21	Uxor Elizabeth Lovell	33	Robert Roberts	18
Robert Duce	18	Rowland Mathew	27	Wm Lake	14
Owen Williams	18	Robert Sprite	30	Richard Iveson	16
Jo: Write	24	Jo: Weston	41	Humfrey Kerby	18
William Clarke	19	James Smith	19	Edward Cokes	17
Edward Halingworth	46	Jo: Smith	19	Henry Morton	20
Richard Pomell	32	Richard Lee	22	James Brett	17
Henry Longsha	23	Wm Seely	29	Tho: Dennis	18
Jo: Bush	22	Edward Plunkett	20	Tho: More	33
Jonathan Franklin	17	Tho: Plunkett	28	Jo: Lawrence	17

Wm Martin		13	Annis Barrat	20	Elizabeth Farmer	20
Richard Phelpe		17	Marie Lambeth	17	Margaret Conway	20
			Ann Mann	17	Grace Walker	34
WOMEN.			Elizabeth Warren	17	Edith Jones	21
Barbarie Reason		20	Ann Skynggle	18	Alice Guy	20
Jane Marshall		21	Alice Champ	20	Mary Spendley	17
Diana Drake		19	Mathew May	21	Ann Gardner	36
Mary Inglish		17	Elizabeth Chambers	20		

21° Maij 1635.

Theis under written names are to be transported to St Christophers, imbarqued in the Mathew of London, Richard Goodladd Mr p' warrant from ye Earle of Carlisle.

Thomas Knight yeres	21	Robert Faucer	40	Jo: Kibie	21
Jo: Hill	18	Miles Coventrie	18	Tho: Garrett	20
Jo: Rawlins	18	Jo: Thomas	14	Jo: Goslinn	20
Francis Penn	22	Tho: Reeve	24	Tho: Milward	18
George Allerton	23	Lewes Anbrey	13	Morgan Brint	19
Rowland Millington	24	James Walker	30	Pierce Stapleton	22
Rich{h} Thomas	40	Tho: Vem	27	Geo: Eaton	27
Roger Thomas	22	Geo. Ball	51	Leonard Hunt	38
Richard Griggson	34	Tho: Gosling	22	Jo: Cave	34
Jo: Bruñing	20	Jo: Palmer	19	Wm Barber	22
Robert Coke	32	James Cotes	21	Jo: Hoddins	50
Clinton Cutler	20	Wm Helaine	21	Alexander Tadde	38
Tho: Turner	25	Mathew Hely	21	Robt. Woodstock	40
Jo: Wood	22	Originall Lowis	28	John Offlent	20
Wm Robinson	26	Jo: Thomson	34	Nic° Watts	18
Edward Bicroft	22	Wm Brookes	25	Richard Brookes	16
Jo: Sturdy	26	Jo: Doe	22	Tho: Hadbie	22
Ant° Netbie	20	Mathew Walker	19	Tho: Reinolds	18
Robert Wendever	25	Walter Collins	18	Darby Hurlie	18
Samvel Trese	20	Jo: Clinton	19	Jo: Hilliard	35
Evan Jones	19	Adam Chesterman	19	Robert Lacie	21
Gabriell Davies	38	Hugh Hallowell	22	Tho: Bell	14
Edward Eeles	20	Wm Salmon	25	Rowland Morton	17
Davie Thomas	40	Jo: Lange	22	James Hide	22
Richard Honibym	31	Richard Lane	28	Richard Nelme	20
Christopher Watson	21	Jo: Greene	29	Tho. Hodges	20
James Hubbard	27	Edward Warren	28	Edward Thomson	18
Wm Stoe	18	Jo: Paple	21	Tho: Williams	18
Mathew Tomlinson	31	Robert Denten	26	Rich{h} Lee	18
Tho: Hall	25	Wm Elvyn	23	Walter Antony	23
Wm Marsh	20	Geo: Toms	20	Charles Caverlie	17
Jo: Hatterton	38	Geo: Swales	19	Tho: Coxson	21
Tho: Terrill	18	Marmaduke Read	25	Tho: Goodwin	30

EMIGRANTS FOR ST. CHRISTOPHERS, &C.

Nicº Wilcocks	21	Wm Knight	13	Geo: Wade	16
Geo: Eeke	26	Antº Williams	14	Jo: Fulford	18
Rich Hubbard	18	Jo: Barloe	22	Geo: Smith	17
Willm Rush	20	Wm Parker	17	Thomas Powell	24
Wm Dorn	22	Jo: Wood	18		
Paul Bottell	32	Jo: Payne	18	**WOMEN.**	
Jo: Boswell	17	Daniell Lee	25	Margaret Prichard	17
Jo: Woodgreene	16	Thoː Powell	21	Jane Burrowe	17
Jo: Harlowe	16	Jo: Smith	22	Katherin Armstrong	20
Robert Warrington	20	Geo: Dodd	17	Mary Barker	12
Jo: Reinolds	20	Robt Sandley	20	Elizabeth Speere	20
Antº True	18	Edward Mawfrey	15		

---

x Junij 1635.

Theis under written names are to be transported to the Bormoodes or Somer-Islands, imbarqued in the Truelove de London. Robert Dennis Mr being examined by the Minister of Gravesend concerning their conformitie to the orders and discipline of the Church of England as it now stands established : And took the oath of Allegeance.

Henry More	19	Wm Paul	20	Nathaniel Willmson	17
Wm Holt	19	Wm Bates	17	Phillipp Wharton	14
Jo: Norman	19	Samvell Short	24	Wm Henry	18
Antº Gilliard	38	Wm Hooper	18	Geo: Saires	12
Robt. Stock	26	Richard Hurt	17	Nicº Gaughton	14
Thoː Foster	27	Willm Wells	17	Edward Hedley	13
Robert Hart	30	Thoː Dene	17	Wm Sares	17
Wm Pendleton	27	Jo: A Negroe	18	Robt Poole	20
James Tayler	28	Jo: Richards	21	Thoː Jones	17
Chri. Hart	20	Antº Bullock	19	Thoː Ervynn	16
Richard Anderson	30	Thomas Bassit	18	Symon Barrott	16
Thoː Richards	24	Edward Aldworth	13	Geo: Calverlie	14
Jo: Norris	18	Edward Vyncent	18	Edward Parnell	16
David Huswith	22	Jo: Truppatt	17	Wm Lee	18
Henry Hill	24	Antº Cooper	17	Wm Tayler	17
Jo: Warren	19	Jo: Lake	16	Edward Gibbs	17
Zeverin Viccars	18	Rich Tayler	16	James Reason	27
Geo: Norman	25	Thoː Mordin	18	Jacob Wilson	18
Gabriell Stockwell	16	Edward Sell	18	Ben: Strange	18
Thoː Torlie	27	Roger Willms	16	Ralph Vennable	21
Edward Goddin	16	Jo: Baylie	18	Thoː Bloes	10
Thoː Dorrell	22	Francis Woodcott	16	Thoː Hedley	11
Richard Cañon	24	Jo: Bee	17	Thoː Thomson	17
Uxor, Elizabeth Cañon	23	Rich Greene	17	Hen: Stonword	13
Barnard Colman	26	Geo: Palmer	18	Samvell Hubbard	16
Chri. Tuke	16	Thoː Smith	14	Thomas Bull	13

Daniell Hammond	12	Francis Hedges	13	Tho: Hall	24
Geo: Morgan	12	Davie Morris	18	Humfrey Smith	14
Jo: Barnes	16	Tho: West	17	Francis Watson	16
Abraham Claxson	17	Hugh Wentworth	44	Katherin White	18
James Aston	22	Ann Taylor	24	Elizabeth Clark	18
Rich Daughton	13	Elizabeth Groves	35	Ellen Burrowes	30
Mathew Steevens	12	Jo: Groves	1 qr.		
Tho: Larkyn	15	Blanch Roberts	20	Jo: Page	33
David Jones	15			Tho: Jennison	21
George Hanmer	24	2 MINISTERS.		Sara Page	31
Roger Hodges	17	Jo: Oxenbridge	24	Sara Page	3
Wm Powell	15	Henry Jennings	24	Mary Page	3 mo.
Sampson Meverill	20			Richard Harris	17
Henry Carter	42	Benjamin Miller	30	Jeffery Wright	18
Jo: Yates	48	Henry Fletcher	35	Samvell Mayo	10
Jo: Browne	16	Edward Staughton	50	Marie Goffe	18
Francis Raynne	10	Josias Forster	43	Jo: Brookes	12

Secundo die Septembris 1635.

Theis under written names are to be transported to St. Christophers: imbarqued in the William and John—Rowland Langram Mr have been examined by the Minister of Gravesend and tooke the oaths of Alleg. and Suprem: die et A° p'.

James Lampley	19	Wm Burnham	21	Samvell Knipe	23
Wm Greene	18	Walter Wall	16	Jo: Watton	25
Henry Daniell	20	Wm Bathoe	18	Jo: Byrall	29
Rowland Davies	20	Tho: Tupper	21	Morris Parry	30
Wm Reddish	20	Wm Baylie	23	Jo: Nayler	20
Edward Brownish	20	Tho: Brookes	21	Edward Nayler	21
Robert Fitt	18	Nathanill Bernard	22	Geo: Noble	22
Richard Lewes	26	Tho: Price	20	Wm Cocks	20
Richard Corie	18	Geo: Frie	19	Martin Sowth	19
Richard Christie	20	Tho: Hart	25	Wm Greenelefe	26
Jo: Brant	24	Mathew Addison	17	Jo: Sawnders	17
Wm Williams	21	Theobald Wall	18	Tho: Hames	16
Christopher Steevenson	19	Robert Richardson	33	John Pinkley	30
Tho: Barnes	20	Robert Leake	38	Robert Thomson	22
Robert Watler	20	Barnabie Brooke	20	Wm Davies	30
Andrew Young	40	Jo: Cock	18	Richard Beare	28
Francis Hudson	36	Nico Cobb	24	Geo: Ford	19
Jo: Parr	19	Jo: Hinson	21	Tho: Lowyun	20
Wm Morley	24	Tho: Ekkersoe	24	Jo: Drake	18
Rich Gavyn	21	Geo: Carter	28	Robert Outmore	38
Tho: Phillipps	35	Rich Harris	26	Hugh Hilton	23
Jo: Willard	16	Henrie Nokes	27	Tho: King	27
Tho: Hanmer	14	Tho: Thompson	28	Lawrence Adderford	26

James Dockkie	17	Nathaniell Simpkins	26	Jo: Kent	23
Ezechell Rennam	15	Wm Procter	26	Robert Lynt	21
Tho: Harden	15	Edward Gressam	17	Edward Bellis	21
Edward Brunt	26	Wm Steevens	21	Tho: Gill	30
Tho: Reinolds	16	Tho: Whithedd	24	Wm Grove	32
Wm Benn	24	Tho: Clark	25	Richard Mason	29
Phillip Skorier	26	Wm Stiffiliynn	16	Manley Richardson	21
Wm Worrall	23	Jo: Bonn	18	Isack Beet	23
Jo: Banson	27	Wm Dunbarr	15	John Pickering	25
Henry Bugland	21	Jo: Morrish	18	Tho: Archbold	19
Jo: Morton	24	Alexander Glover	37	Mathew Wells	28
Jo: Ditchfield	22	Edward King	25		

Tricessimo die Septembris 1635.

Aboard the Dorsst John Flower Mr bound for ye Bormodes.

John Redford	16	Tho: Stokes	30	Edward Simpson	13
Robert Ramsey	15	Wm Rosden	16	Edward Grubthorn	14
John Williams	16	Nathaniell West	15	Jonas Goldenham	16
Willm Elliston	13	Jo: Donn	14	Judith Bagley	53
Lubas Wright	16	Edward Edwynn	15	John Glassenden	14
Humfrey Holt	18	Jo: Sell	15	Wm Harding	30
Tho: Joyner	16	Tho: Ireland	10	Uxor Sarah Harding	30
Rich Tregagell	18	Edward Davies	17	Henry Rosse	31
Jo: Loe	18	Edward Simpson	13	Tymothie Pynder	26
Josua Woodcock	11	Edward Aldin	17	Margaret Pynder	41
Robert Fisher	10	Tho: Atkins	16	Jane Dart	17
Tho Sharp	17	Tho: Riley	16	Geo: Tuck	40
Jo: Rowland	21	Wm Barnes	15	Ezia Vyntent	30
Wm Wheeler	22	Jo: Day	16	Uxor Mathew	30
Wm Pennington	18	Wm Barrith	16	Minister Daniell Wite	30
Jo: Mathews	16	Jo: Tustin	16	Sampson Lort	30
Robert Vardell	20	Jo: Necklin	17	Jo: Miller	47
Jo: Heth	21	Jo: Harkwood	20	John Johnson	23
Nathaniell Bonnick	16	Humfrey Kemp	16	Richard Jennings	35
Jo: Denman	14	David Thomas	26	Uxor Sara Jennings	18
Tho: More	18	Willm Alburie	15	Richard Palmer	30
Wm Bruister	17	Arthur Thorne	33	Uxor Ellis Palmer	21
George Hubbard	16	Wm Cheeseman	20	Tho: Griffin	32
Edw: Middleton	15	John Mitchell	20	Ann Griffin	35
Francis Russell	23	John Casson	18	Robert Ridley	23
James Rising	18	Alexander Brabant	30	Elizabeth Ridley,	30
Geo: Absolon	16	Henry Fulcock	15	Edward Chaplin	20
Jo: Mosdell	24	Jo: Mansfield	19	Wm Casse	19
Wm Stocker	19	Willm Craft	15	Peternell Nowell	46
Edward Morris	18	Richard Haldin	14	Christian Wellman	43
Wm Thomas	17	Geo. Palmer	27	Eliz: Aldworth	15
Rich Bunting	17	Wm Simpson	17		

EMIGRANTS FOR ST. CHRISTOPHERS, &C.

2° die Octobris 1635.

Aboard the John of London James Waymoth Mʳ bound to St Christophers.

John Batcheller	26	Willm̄ Richardson	24	Jo: Sherlock	20
Samvell Parker	19	Edward Mekins	18	Tho: Frost	28
Tho: James	25	Jo: Clymer	30	Lewes Evans	25
Chri. Thomson	21	Richard Evans	21	Jo: Thomson	19
Alexander Fleetwood	19	Henrie Feeld	25	Richard Townsend	19
Walter Lee	21	Henrie Radford	20	Mary Goodwin	18
Edward Dodson	21	Jo: Henman	19	Jane Goodwyn	20
Gilbert Clark	19	Tho: Walker	19	Martha Lilliot	20
Geo: Heelis	19	Jo: Mulleneux	24	Elizabeth Murrin	21
Richard Elmes	21	Oswell Metcalf	22	Joan Hill	21
Richard Smith	22	Edward Cooke	22	Elizabeth Freeman	18

13° die Octobris 1635.

Aboard the Amitie George Downes Mʳ bound to Sᵗ Christophʳˢ.

Isack Drake	25	George Coop'	20	John Jack	27
Richard Iveson	24	Mathew Preston	22	Tho: Yott	24
Robert Barne	33	John Pynkston	27	John Teirrer	24
Tho: Hernden	23	Wᵐ Geies	18	John Farmer	24
Edward Farr	28	Willm̄ Vbank	20	Wᵐ Daughten	20
Wᵐ Burrowe	19	Charles Parker	18	Ricʰ Skynner	20
Tho: Brewyun	24	James Leachman	22	Wᵐ Egerton	20
Marmaduke Borne	21	Wᵐ Cartwrite	18	James Makyn	20
Willm Creswell	22	Richard West-Garrett	20	Wᵐ Harris	20
Henrie Hodgskynns	19	Wᵐ Harris	16	Bastian Petite	23
Robert Payne	21	Jer: Nicholls	16	John Warren	20
George Hatrell	32	Tho: Rodes	20	Ricʰ Phinnei	30
Jo: Hippsley	19	Jo: Boughei	21	James Briggs	25
Willm̄ Stanley	22	Edward Grindall	21	John Musick	19
John Snape	22	Jo: Vaughan	23	Jo: Griddick	16
Isack Buck	33	Jo: Goddın	20	Wᵐ Davies	40
Walter Ellitt	20	Richard Larkyn	32	Robt Heath	30
Aymies Halfyard	19	Richard Bodman	23	Tho: Baggelay	24
Oliver Johnes	25	Tho: Molton	20	William Yateman	25
John Smith	23	David Owen	26	Richard Grind	11
Hamblet Sankey	22	Henrie Rowles	22	Wᵐ Galler	20
Edward Porter	21	Nicᵒ Alford	28	Robert Downe	35
Tho. Galley	20	Samvell Sakell	23	John Hye	36
Tho: Pitts	24	Robert Jones	30	Edward Webb	17
Jo: Thomson	25	Jo: Browne	33	James Johnson	28
Richard Webster	24	Peter Salmon	20	John Avery	22
Lewes Jones	20	Jo: Saunderson	23	Daniell Cannelly	20
John Coombes	26	Robert Rolfe	23	Rice Poke	30

EMIGRANTS FOR ST. CHRISTOPHERS, &C.

Roger James	29	Wm Rule	20	Alice Barker	30
James Curtis	18	—		Patient White	44
Clement Haines	22	Mary Wynd	18	Isack and Jacob } Twynns	2
John Fynn	22	Margaret Coles	21		
Wm Goff	30	Marie Merriton	21	Judith Lloyd	18
Andrew White	11	Kat: Brewett	16	Marie Maxwell	21
John Billinghurst	24	Ellen Channce	21		
Morrice Davie	24	Ann Palmer	29		

20 Novembris 1635.

Theis under written names are to be transported to the Barbadoes, imbarqued in the Expedition, Peter Blackler M^r. The Men have taken the oaths of Allegeance and Supremacie. And have been examined by the minister of the Towne of Gravesend touching their Conformitie to the ord^{rs} and discipline of the Church of England die et A° prd.

Minist^r Nicholas Bloxā als Jagles yeres	31	John Mann	21	Willm Tayler	26
Abram Holland	19	Tho: Peacock	17	John Parlin	21
Thomas Hudson	16	Edward Steevens	53	Wm Jackson	33
Blackwell Lawrence	16	Thomas Weekes	23	John Medgley	21
Leonard Briggins	17	Hugh Cheswood	21	Wm Wreuch	21
Thomas Clark	27	Jo: Coert	21	Robert Hurt	19
Morgan Jenkins	32	John Pike	30	James Farebank	26
Ric^h Pratt	18	George Blacklock	32	Henrie Berrisford	32
Tho: Freeman	19	John Coleman	40	James Nettleton	22
Willm Greefeson	26	Wm Watts	28	Thomas Armitage	24
Richard Wartumbee	21	John Bonner	18	Francis Mann	19
Henry Bryan	21	Willm Snignell	18	John Felkynn	20
Hugh Dawson	18	Tho: Hobin	20	John Jones	20
Mathew Beads	19	Francis Barnit	23	Richard Lightbound	22
Charles Lambert	23	Willm̄ Buckley	26	Christopher Hartlie	19
Jo: Lake	18	John Clark	16	Tho: Wood	23
Jo: Smith	18	Phillipp Morlin	21	Henrie Godfrie	36
Anthony Hutchins	32	Henry Rawlins	25	Tho: Palmer	19
Willm Gibson	19	Jo: Rudge	42	Jo: Humfrey	20
Jo: Williams	17	Edward Evans	22	John Smith	22
William Steward	21	John Hownsefield	20	Ambrose Greene	23
John Pierce	18	Tho: Davie	20	Jo: Hilliard	18
Hugh Evans	18	Henry Gowde	19	Jo: Browne	26
Brian Aston	21	Wm Mellison	25	Willm Warr	19
Nicholas Collon	19	John York	26	Mathew Wilkinson	18
Henry Field	24	Wm Carpenter	19	Mathew Gibbons	20
Richard Smith	20	John Wynter	23	Wm Audley	18
John Knowles	27	Jo: Waller	17	James Kingston	22
John Dickenson	24	John Sumes	20	Ric^h Smart	20
		John Heron	20	Wm Walters	26

EMIGRANTS FOR ST. CHRISTOPHERS, &C.

Tho: Davies	23	Peter Croningburk	20	James Smith	24
Nathaniell Nordin	46	Jo: Hall	29	Nic° Flutter	27
Wm Pitt	25	Jo: Compton	26	Nic° Whithedd	24
Jo: Chater	17	Clement Backford	30	Wm Hinkynn	26
Jo: Chapman	24	Robert Browne	18	Thomas Gilbert	26
Geo: Sterry	24	John Key	32	Richard Seabright	21
Abram Cheynei	22	Howell Pryce	25	Robert Greenewood	18
Jo: Sturton	18	Edward Aston	32	Anthony Ashmore	33
Jo: Edens	19	Robt Edwards	38	Launcelott Bromley	44
Lawrence Brock	18	Richard Ash	24	Peter Spencer	15
Ric^h Best	18	John Medley	26	Thomas Phipps	15
Robert Hobbs	26	Thomas King	24	Davie Thomas	20
Peter Jones	30	Richard Snowe	28	Willm Greene	23
Wm Topleife	18	Robert Filborne	18	Jo: Watts	20
Jo: Robinson	19	Pierce Morgan	23	Wm Lock	21
Morrice Jones	21	Jo: Williams	17	George Leas	20
Henry Stint	18	Nic° Brogan	28	John Spencer	19
Josias Weston	25	Ant° Smith	18	Henry Antony	19
Francis Birkenhedd	24	John Spenceley	24	James Fassitt	34
Edward Jones	29	Mathew Shore	46	Henry Ellotts	23
Ellis Williams	18	Thomas St Parlin	19	Henry Coke	28
Wm Tayler	40	Dorothy Symonds	40	Richard Benes	25
Tho: Burnham	18	Mary Lupton	30	Wm Cosson	20
Joseph Boyce	24	Ric^h Horne	22	Wm Thomson	20
Jo: Rainescroft	23	John Newton	29	Thomas Usherwood	28
Henrie Bostock	19	Thomas Cowdell	17	Wm Haning	30
Jefferie Shipp	24	Richard Gibson	25	John Goad	22
Wm Brooke	26	Nicholas Nevell	19	Richard Moncaster	32
Lanncelott Lacon	32	George Tayler	20	John Chesting	21
Wm Plomer	23	Wm Goad	21	Roger Sanford	35
Wm Sheicrofte	17	Wm Marritt	26	Wm Cornwell	20
Wm Coke	18	Roger Eritage	22	Wm Gosselin	21
Jo: Jennings	18	Davie Dodderidge	20	Jo: Coop'	21
Tho: Ossebrooke	27	George Fullwood	19	Wm Price	22
Jo: Davenport	30	Ric^h Hamis	21	Sam: Skynner	22
Geo: Burton	23	Ralph Webster	20	Robt. Dunstarr	34
Wm Morgan	20	Tho: Robinson	15	Richard Buck	24
Davie Thomas	20	Joseph Thomlinson	26	Nic° Lynton	22
Ric^h Hannis	21	Baltazar Dederix	26		

19 Dec: 1635.

Theis under-written names are to be transported to the Barbadoes imbarqued in the Falcon Tho: Irish M^r the Men have been examined by the Minister of the Towne of Grauesend touching their conformitie to the Church discipline of England: And also haue taken the Oaths of Alleg': and Suprem die et A° pr^d

EMIGRANTS FOR ST. CHRISTOPHERS, &C.

Arnold Ownstedd yeres	30	James Spencer	25	Jo: Burkett	21
Tho: Skyddell	28	Jo: Chubnell	21	Tho: Harrwell	29
Ant° Cadwold	23	Wᵐ Gunter	22	Gregorie Booth	18
Phillipp Miller	21	Jo: Thurrogood	20	Edward Howe	19
Maximillian Prichard	20	Tho: Greene	16	Robt Clarke	18
Tho: Tisfin	28	Richard Richardson	36	Francis Martin	18
Jo: Butler	21	Rebecca Burgis	17	Tho: Webb	22
Phines Trusedell	18	Richard Panke	19	Jo: Scott	42
Bryan Cowley	30	Leonard Robinson	20	Tho: Evans	23
Jo: Mason	19	Francis Buck	20	Wᵐ Phillips	28
Robert Harris	42	John Hogg	21	James Cotesworth	21
Abram Shawe	20	Robert Symper	20	Ellinn Robb	27
Geo: Sabyn	21	Tho: Page	20	filia Elizabeth Robb	7
Wᵐ Cartwrite	23	Dennis Britten	20	Tho: Clark	27
Nathan Murfitt	23	Jo: Rogers	18		
Jo: Barnett	20	James Wolton	22		

25 decembris 1635.

Theis under-written names passed in a Catch to the Downes; and were put aboard the aforesaid shipp.

Tho: Davies	17	Griffinn Evans	40	Wᵐ Coñisby	31
Henry Benson	19	James Terrill	20	Robert Tissall	30
Jo: Welsh	35	Elizabeth Cossen	25	Tristram Ford	21
Henry Southward	20	Jane Hickles	25	Elias Carpenter	20
Ricʰ Newbolt	28	Henry Van Luccom	24	Richard Hames	18
Lawrence Keysie	28	Jo: King	30	Thomas Streter	21
James Robinson	15	Wᵐ Flatter	18	James Lee	28
Ant° Pope	28	Jo: Weston	27		
Jo: Lee	30	Tho: Clark	28		

INDEX OF NAMES OF PASSENGERS.

NOTE.—Variations of the same names, are usually given under the most common mode of spelling them.

A.

Abbott, 19, 69, 102
Abdy, 36
Absolon, 110
Adams, 29, 33, 39, 102
Adderford, 109
Addison, 109
Aiers, 49
Akyers, 100
Albon, 42
Alburie, 110
Alcock, 36, 60
Aldburg, 54
Aldin, 110
Aldworth, 108, 110
Alford, 111
Allen, 33, 81
Allerton, 86, 107
Alley, 35
Alliday, 102
Allin, 99, 100, 103
Allis, 12
Almond, 34
Almy, 34
Alsopp, 23, 30
Alxarson, 45
Ambrey, 104
Ames, 49
Anbrey, 107
Anderson, 75, 76, 101, 105, 106, 108
Andrews, 24, 56
Androwe, 105
Anthony, 70, 71
Antony, 107, 113
Antram, 56
Antrobuss, 16
Archbold, 110
Armitage, 112
Armstrong, 108
Arnold, 36, 99
Arres, 45
Arthur, 65
Ash, 78, 99, 113

Ashbey, 32
Ashmore, 113
Ashurst, 106
Aston, 103, 109, 112, 113
Astwood, 17
Atherson, 26
Atkins, 106, 110
Atkinson, 102, 104
Atwood, 18, 23
Audley, 112
Austin, 60, 83
Avery, 70, 105, 111
Awbrey, 104
Ayres, 26, 27

B.

Baalam, 77
Bachelor, 85
Backford, 113
Bacon, 20, 105
Badcocke, 66
Badland, 65
Bagin, 102
Bagley, 110, 111
Baker, 16, 27, 30, 44, 49, 100, 103, 104
Baldwin, 38, 77
Ball, 107
Ballard, 39, 70
Banes, 39, 74
Banks, 102, 106
Banshott, 60
Banson, 110
Barber, 14, 107
Barcrofte, 12
Barker, 86, 108, 112
Barloe, 108
Barnard, 100
Barnes, 77, 102, 105, 109, 110, 111
Barnett, 114
Barnıt, 112
Barran, 105
Barret, 26, 105, 107

Barrith, 110
Barrott, 108
Barry, 66
Bartlett, 12, 70
Barton, 50, 104
Basher, 101
Bassett, 14, 34, 86, 103, 106, 108
Batcheller, 111
Bates, 18, 27, 108
Bathe, 103
Bathoe, 109
Batt, 56, 60
Batter, 56
Baunsh, 59
Baxter, 80
Bayley, 58, 61
Baylie, 41, 108, 109
Bead, 101, 112
Beale, 31, 80
Beames, 75
Beamond, 24
Bearheik, 78
Bearce, 59
Beardsley, 16
Beardes, 26
Beare, 109
Beaton, 106
Beck, 40
Beckett, 55, 103
Bedding, 105
Beddle, 102
Bedlam, 105
Bee, 108
Beeresto, 43
Beet, 110
Beetes, 53
Beer, 74
Befford, 106
Belcher, 23, 36
Bell, 105, 107
Bellis, 110
Bellowes, 19
Belton, 103

Beme, 74
Benes, 113
Benjamin, 12
Benne, 76, 110
Bennet, 28, 39, 105
Benning, 105
Benson, 100, 114
Benstedd, 106
Bent, 58
Bentley, 39, 43, 78
Beomont, 29
Bereere, 75
Bernard, 51, 52, 53, 54, 109
Berkynn, 102
Berrisford, 112
Berry, 87
Bertie, 69
Besbeech, 84
Bessy, 39
Best, 84, 113
Bewlie, 24
Bicron, 107
Biddleston, 103
Bidgood, 59
Bidlcombe, 57
Bigg, 27
Bigges, 40
Bigmore, 72
Bill, 17, 18, 67
Billinghurst, 112
Bills, 41
Bingham, 103
Binson, 59
Bird, 23
Birkenhedd, 113
Bitton, 26
Blacke, 75
Blackgrove, 99
Blackley, 41
Blacklocke, 112
Blackwell, 43
Blackstone, 60
Blades, 100, 101
Blake, 58
Blanford, 57
Blason, 26
Bliss, 103
Blodgett, 25
Bloes, 108
Bloomfield, 51, 52
Blosse, 53, 54
Blowar, 43
Bloxsall, 104
Bodman, 111
Bolt, 103
Bolton, 105
Boney, 83
Bonn, 110
Bonner, 112
Bonnick, 110
Boone, 102

Booth, 114
Borden, 30
Borebancke, 33
Borinthon, 66
Borne, 99, 111
Borrow, 49
Bortes, 78
Borthamer, 78
Bostock, 113
Bouwell, 108
Bottell, 108
Boughei, 111
Boules, 77
Boulle, 45
Bourk, 105
Bowdoin, 65
Bowes, 99
Bownd, 100
Boy, 76
Boyce, 67, 113
Boyden, 53
Boyn, 75, 76
Boykett, 85
Boylston, 37
Braban, 102
Brahant, 110
Bracey, 25
Bradford, 86
Bradstreet, 14, 51, 52
Brand, 77
Brane, 36
Brant, 109
Brett, 106
Brewer, 12, 88
Brewett, 112
Brewster, 88
Brewyun, 111
Bridgen, 84
Bridges, 39, 104
Brigges, 40, 111
Briggins, 112
Brigham, 25
Brinsley, 77
Brint, 107
Britten, 114
Brocke, 28, 113
Brodley, 19
Brogan, 113
Bromby, 103
Bromley, 113
Brook, 105
Brooke, 25, 29, 35, 83, 107, 109, 113
Broome, 43
Broomer, 23, 25
Brow, 75
Brown, 50
Browne, 12, 25, 27, 30, 31, 33, 41, 43, 44, 48, 55, 56, 70, 101, 106, 109, 111, 112, 113

Brownell, 74
Brownish, 109
Brownley, 102
Broughton, 106
Bruister, 110
Brumwell, 103
Bruning, 107
Brunt, 99, 110
Bruster, 105
Bruton, 100
Bryan, 100, 112
Bryant, 67
Buckanen, 75
Buck, 26, 40, 81, 111, 113, 114
Buckland, 106
Buckiey, 24, 26, 112
Buckrum, 87
Bugbye, 53, 54
Bugland, 110
Bulkley, 29
Bull, 22, 39, 42, 103, 104, 108
Bullman, 106
Bullock, 27, 30, 108
Bunce, 103
Bundick, 17
Bundocke, 15, 19
Bunting, 110
Bunystedd, 100
Burche, 106
Burchard, 43
Burcherd, 42
Burden, 35
Burges, 49, 114
Burkell, 114
Burlace, 66
Burnham, 109, 113
Burrowes, 66, 109
Burrow, 23, 108, 111
Burt, 34, 36, 99, 103
Burtes, 39
Burton, 105, 106, 113
Burules, 40
Busbie, 45
Bush, 106
Bushell, 36
Bushnell, 18, 19
Busket, 14
Bussell, 106
Bustells, 78
Butler, 56, 85, 86, 87, 114
Butterworth, 87
Butterrick, 19, 24
Buttolph, 29
Buttry, 40
Byham, 35
Byley, 60
Byrall, 109

INDEX OF NAMES OF PASSENGERS. 117

C.

Caddy, 100
Cadwold, 114
Calland. 106
Calle, 85
Calverhe, 108
Camell, 75
Cammion, 99
Caunell, 75
Cannelly, 111
Canon, 108
Cant, 101
Cappledyke, 99
Carey. 86
Carkill, 67
Carmackhell, 76
Carpenter, 24, 56, 60, 86, 88, 99, 112, 114
Carr. 30, 36, 105
Carrington. 12
Carter, 16, 17, 65, 68, 75, 99, 102, 109
Cartrack, 23
Cartwright, 101, 111, 114
Carver, 46, 88
Casse, 110
Casseday, 100
Casson, 110
Cave, 107
Caverlie, 107
Cawdle, 104
Cawood, 105
Chaddock, 104
Chamberlin, 80
Chambers, 42, 107
Chamblis, 93
Champ, 107
Champion, 83
Chandler, 87
Channce, 112
Chaplin, 27, 110
Chapman, 22, 48, 102, 103, 113
Chappell, 14
Charles, 87
Chater, 113
Checkley, 50
Cheeseman, 110
Chenall, 40
Chesterman, 107
Chesting, 113
Cheswood, 112
Cheynei, 113
Chingelton, 86
Chippfield, 42
Chitting, 99
Chittingden, 25
Chitwood, 16
Christie, 109
Chubbuck, 79
Chubnell, 114

Church, 58, 102, 103, 106
Churchman, 12
Clark, 12, 18, 42, 47, 65, 70, 77, 78, 100, 101, 102, 103 106, 109, 110, 111, 112, 114
Claxson, 109
Clearke, 51, 53, 54
Clemens, 88
Clement, 55, 99
Clere, 101
Clerke, 101
Clevin, 42
Clewston, 74
Cliffe, 99
Clifford, 23
Clinton. 100, 107
Cluffe, 21
Clymer, 111j
Cobb, 109
Cobbett, 28
Cobham, 100
Cocke, 37, 65, 109
Cockey, 99
Cockman, 103
Cockram, 50
Codmore, 87
Coe, 23
Coehon, 74
Coert, 112
Coke, 19, 35, 99, 102, 103, 104, 105, 106, 107, 113
Coker, 70
Colborne, 39
Colbron, 39
Colburne, 39
Cole, 23, 41, 58, 71, 83, 106, 112
Coleman, 78, 112
Collie, 101
Collingworth. 106
Collins, 35, 78, 107
Collon, 112
Colman, 56, 108
Comberback, 45
Compton, 113
Conasley, 13
Conisby, 114
Conly, 105
Conniers, 100
Conny, 99
Connyer, 105
Conway, 107
Cooe, 53, 55
Cooke, 36, 111
Cooleman, 78, 85
Coombes, 111
Coop, 21, 23, 111, 113
Cooper, 14, 15, 16, 24, 48, 79, 80, 104, 108
Cope, 35

Copeland, 77
Coose, 67
Corfer, 100
Corie, 109
Cornew, 66
Cornwell, 113
Corrington, 26
Cossens, 114
Cosson, 113
Cotes, 107
Cotesworth, 114
Cottington, 69
Cottle, 58
Courser, 30
Courtney, 67
Courtis, 56
Coussens, 56
Covell, 34
Coventry, 69, 107
Cowdell, 113
Cowley, 114
Coxsall, 12
Coxson, 107
Crackston, 87
Craddock, 19
Craft, 110
Cragg, 74
Cragon, 74
Crakins, 104
Crane, 77
Crapp, 100
Creswell, 111
Crew, 103
Cribb, 14, 106
Crispin, 103
Crockford, 76
Crofts, 105
Crome, 106
Croningburk, 113
Croome, 74
Crosby, 25, 103
Cross, 26, 51
Crosshone, 75
Crowder, 100, 102
Crowley, 24
Crullings, 87
Cullens, 87
Cullimor, 101
Curke, 65
Curmiekhell, 75
Curtis, 12, 29, 103, 112
Cushing, 79, 80
Cushman, 86
Cutler, 82, 102, 107
Cutting, 51, 52

D.

Dabh, 106
Dabbin, 65
Dales, 104, 105
Dallinger, 103

INDEX OF NAMES OF PASSENGERS.

Dalton, 26
Damand, 23
Dane, 30, 102
Danell, 49
Daniell. 26, 109
Darno. 39
Dart, 110
Daughton, 109, 111
Davenport, 113
Davers, 103
David, 106
Davie, 112
Davies, 15, 26, 27, 40, 56, 71, 99, 100, 102, 105, 107, 109, 110, 111, 113, 114
Davison, 77
Davis, 58, 59
Daues, 40
Dawes, 18
Dawson, 102, 112
Day, 17, 30, 51, 110
Dayes, 100
Deane, 21
Dederix, 113
Dell, 74
Dellahay, 106
Dench, 106
Dene, 101, 108
Deugle, 75
Denman, 110
Dennis, 103, 106
Denny, 33
Dent, 103
Denten, 107
Depark, 101
Derborn, 100
Desbrough, 17
Devotion, 36
Dexter, 18
Deyking, 36
Dickenson, 104, 112
Dickerson, 48
Dingby, 86
Dingley, 57
Disherd, 103
Ditchfield, 110
Dix, 26, 46
Dixon, 105
Dixson, 48
Dockhie, 110
Dodd, 36, 108
Dodderidge, 100, 113
Dodson, 111
Doc. 107
Doged. 50
Done. 43
Donley, 59
Donn, 39, 110
Dorifall. 51
Dorn, 108
Durrell, 108

Dounard, 20
Dow, 47
Downe, 111
Dowsell, 104
Drake, 107, 109, 111
Drap, 53, 103
Draper, 105
Dreadd, 100
Drew, 100
Drewrie, 33
Drinker, 36
Driver, 34, 106
Duce, 106
Duhurst, 38
Duke, 21
Dukharth, 102
Dulen, 74
Dummer, 61
Dunbar, 110
Dunn, 65
Dunstan, 113
Durdal, 60
Dustan, 66
Dye, 103
Dyer, 14
Dymond, 100
Dynley, 105

E.

Eaarle, 77
Early, 71
Easmen, 58
Easton, 70
Eaton, 23, 85, 100, 107
Edens, 113
Edminsteire. 74
Edmonds, 99
Edwards, 42, 66, 71, 77, 113
Edwynn, 110
Edye, 42, 65
Eeke, 108
Eeles, 107
Egerton, 111
Ekhersoe, 109
Ellerton, 101
Ellgate, 101
Elliott, 17, 71
Ellis, 34, 86, 88
Elliston, 110
Ellitt, 111
Ellmer, 12
Ellotts, 113
Ellvyn, 99
Ellwood, 43
Elmes, 21, 111
Elson, 103
Elvyn, 107
Emerson. 36
Emery, 56
English. 74, 76
Epps, 38

Eritage, 113
Erle, 100
Erskine, 69
Ervynn, 108
Estplyun, 105
Etherington, 99
Evans, 86, 102, 103, 105, 111, 112, 114
Evered, 56
Everie, 101
Ewell, 83
Ewer, 31
Eyre, 47

F.

Faber, 28
Fabin, 29
Fairfield, 87
Faldoe, 18
Fall, 103
Fane, 106
Fannell, 83
Farebank, 112
Farebrother, 39
Farfason, 74
Farman, 40
Farmer, 102, 107, 111
Farr, 111
Farren, 65
Farring, 106
Farrington, 15, 16
Farron, 106
Farronds, 19
Farrow, 79
Fassitt, 113
Faucer, 107
Faux, 100
Fay, 77
Fearfax, 102
Feeld, 111
Feld, 104
Felkynn, 112
Felloe, 16
Felver, 104
Fenn, 19
Fenner, 43
Fennick, 39
Ferrier, 87
Ferring, 81
Field. 56, 112
Fifield, 71
Filborn, 113
Fillingham, 48
Finch, 88
Firman, 51
Fish, 105
Fisher, 102, 110
Fitch, 38, 39, 40
Fitt, 109
Flade, 99
Flaming, 106
Flatter, 114

INDEX OF NAMES OF PASSENGERS. 119

Fleetwood, 111
Flege, 46
Fleming, 26
Fletcher, 86, 99, 109
Flitcroft, 103
Fludd, 35, 106
Flutter, 113
Fokar, 26
Fookes, 99
Ford, 25, 64, 109, 114
Forgine, 66
Forster, 109
Forten, 42
Fossein, 74
Foster, 27, 34, 71, 108
Foulfoot, 14
Foulsham, 80, 82
Fountaine, 35
Fowle, 24
Fowler, 70, 100
Fowlsom, 50
Fox, 34, 100
Franklin, 70, 106
Frazill, 105
Frebourne, 53, 54
Free, 100
Freeman, 33, 34, 36, 42, 111, 112
French, 37, 67, 102
Frethy, 65
Fresell, 75
Frost, 65, 111
Fry, 60, 109
Fryrne, 99
Fulcock, 110
Fulford, 108
Fuller, 18, 29, 86, 88
Fullwood, 113
Fynn, 112

G.

Gale, 105
Galler, 111
Galley, 111
Galloway, 106
Gane, 100
Garde, 106
Gardner, 27, 39, 41, 107
Garnett, 53
Gamlin, 11
Garrard, 105
Garret, 102, 105, 107
Gass, 102
Gates, 80
Gaton, 100
Gaughton, 108
Gault, 49
Gavyn, 109
Gedney, 45, 49
Gee, 82
Geere, 31

Geies, 111
Gerden, 103
Gibbert, 78
Gibbins, 24
Gibbons, 77, 112
Gibbs, 79, 108
Gibson, 100, 102, 112, 113
Giddins, 16
Giggon, 103
Gilbert, 113
Gilby, 100
Gilder, 103
Gildingwater, 106
Gill, 110
Gillam, 36
Gillett, 70
Gilliard, 108
Gillies, 87
Gillman, 80
Gilson, 25, 106
Glade, 99
Gladwell, 26
Glascock, 86
Glassenden, 110
Glover, 51, 110
Glower, 12
Goad, 38, 113
Goadby, 17
Goard, 28, 29
Goare, 28
Godhert, 86
Goddard, 56
Goddar, 88
Goddin, 105, 108, 111
Godfrie, 68
Godfrey, 70, 112
Goffe, 39, 109, 112
Gold, 18, 20, 103
Goldenham, 110
Goldham, 104
Golding, 105
Goldingham, 101
Goldsworth, 103
Gonn, 39
Good, 60
Goodall, 51, 53, 86
Gooden, 104
Goodenowe, 58, 77
Goodhue, 40
Goodin, 48
Goodman, 106
Goodwyn, 12, 104, 107, 111
Gordon, 24, 75, 76
Gosling, 107
Gosselin, 113
Gould, 32
Gouldinge, 68
Gouldson, 51, 53
Gowde, 112
Granger, 99
Grant, 12, 74, 75

Graunt, 75, 76
Graves. 33, 42
Gray, 88, 102
Greealy, 102
Greefeson, 112
Greene, 12, 16, 17, 26, 53, 54, 56, 73, 74, 99, 105, 106, 107, 108, 109, 112, 113, 114
Greenelefe, 109
Greenly, 103
Greenoway, 22
Greenwood, 100, 102, 113
Greenwich, 106
Grenfield, 49
Gressam, 110
Griddick, 111
Griffin, 66, 104, 110
Griffiths, 35
Griffs, 100
Griggs, 15
Griggson, 99, 107
Grind, 111
Grindall, 111
Ground, 100
Grover, 43
Groves, 109, 110
Grubb, 105
Grubthorn, 110
Grynwich, 86
Gualmay, 103
Gullifer, 105
Gunn, 74
Gunter, 43, 114
Gurden, 74
Gurge, 67
Gurner, 75
Gutsall, 33
Guy, 58, 107

H.

Hackwell, 26
Hadbie, 107
Hadborne, 33
Hadwell, 78
Haford, 16
Haies, 100, 102
Haile, 43
Haines, 112
Haldin, 110
Halford, 15
Halfyard, 111
Hall, 85, 107, 109, 113
Haloway, 103
Halowell, 107
Halsey, 29
Halworthy, 78
Hamblen, 104
Hame, 76, 101, 109, 114
Hamilton, 75, 76
Hamis, 113
Hamond, 53, 54, 101, 104, 109

INDEX OF NAMES OF PASSENGERS.

Hanbury, 18
Hands, 101, 103
Hanford, 21
Hangert, 59
Haning, 113
Hanmer, 109
Hannis, 113
Hanoman, 74
Hansby, 100
Hapley, 103
Harbert, 33
Harden, 110
Harding, 29, 105, 110
Hardy, 86, 106
Harkwood, 110
Harlackenden, 36
Harlowe, 108
Harman, 41
Harris, 11, 14, 68, 84, 100, 103, 105, 109, 111, 114
Harrison, 38, 100
Harron, 75
Harrowig, 104
Harrwell, 114
Hart, 11, 33, 40, 46, 68, 108, 109
Hartforde, 101
Hartley, 105, 112
Harvey, 16
Harwood, 67, 100
Hassard, 104
Hassel, 21
Hastings, 104
Hatch, 83
Hatfield, 87
Hathaway, 35, 40, 51
Hathorne, 101
Hatrell, 111
Hatterton, 107
Hatton, 50
Haulton, 53
Haus, 28
Hausen, 87
Haward, 54
Hawes, 43, 56
Hawk, 81
Hawkins, 21, 23, 67, 106
Hawkseworth, 15
Hayman, 100
Hayne, 57
Hayward, 11, 15, 21, 50, 105
Hazel, 103
Heath, 12, 42, 111
Hedeicke, 75
Hedges, 109
Hedley, 108
Hedsall, 20
Heelis, 111
Helaine, 107
Hely, 107
Henman, 111

Henry, 108
Henson, 103
Hepworth, 101
Hernden, 111
Heron, 112
Herring, 106
Herrnhill, 33
Heth, 110
Hewlett, 70, 71
Heylei, 15
Heyward, 83
Hibbens, 71, 103
Hickless, 114
Hide, 56, 107
Hidrecke, 76
Higdon, 56
Higgins, 99
Highen, 75
Hill, 11, 38, 40, 68, 100, 103, 106, 107, 108, 111
Hilliard, 107, 112
Hillman, 36
Hilton, 105, 109
Hinkley, 83
Hinkynn, 113
Hinne, 75
Hinson, 109
Hippsley, 111
Hitchcock, 23
Hiter, 100
Hobart, 79
Hobbs, 78, 104, 113
Hobin, 112
Hobson, 100
Hocksley, 68
Hoddins, 107
Hodges, 19, 107, 109
Hodgkynns, 111
Hodgson, 100
Hoeman, 32
Hogg, 74, 76, 114
Holburd, 103
Holder, 77
Holdred, 19
Holdsworth, 105
Holland, 99, 112
Hollinby, 102
Hollingsworth, 40, 106
Holliock, 34
Hollis, 102
Holloway, 28, 105
Holly, 35
Holmar, 12
Holmes, 99, 100, 102
Holt, 56, 108, 110
Homes, 45, 77
Honihym, 107
Hookham, 106
Hooper, 39, 108
Hopgood, 77
Hoppine, 68

Hopwood, 103
Horne, 113
Horsham, 104
Horwood, 14
Hosmer, 20
Houghton, 26, 32
Houlding, 53
Houseman, 102, 106
How, 75
Howe, 43, 104, 114
Hownesfield, 112
Howse, 106
Howson, 14
Hoyt, 86, 88
Hubbard, 23, 27, 39, 40, 42, 101, 107, 108, 110
Huchinson, 60
Huckle, 106
Hudson 24, 74, 75, 99, 109, 112
Huett, 102
Hughes, 100, 106
Hull, 29, 42
Hune, 75
Humfrey, 112
Hunt, 107
Hunter, 100
Hurlie, 107
Hurt, 108, 112
Huswith, 108
Hutchins, 100, 112
Hutchinson, 105
Hutley, 42
Hye, 111
Hynd, 103
Hywood, 102

I.

Iles, 100
Ilsbey, 59
Ingles, 56
Inglish, 107
Ingram, 40
Ireland, 26, 110
Ireson, 34
Isaack, 51
Ives, 43
Iveson, 102, 106, 111

J.

Jacson, 76
Jack, 111
Jackson, 23, 29, 38, 40, 74, 100, 101, 102, 105, 106, 112
Jacob, 70, 79
Jagles, 112
Jago, 101
Jameson, 76
James, 12, 80, 81, 111, 112
Jamnell, 74
Jarman, 29

INDEX OF NAMES OF PASSENGERS.

Jay, 15
Jeffries, 30
Jeller, 74
Jenkins, 43, 112
Jenkynn, 39, 100
Jenler, 74
Jenne, 86
Jennings, 53, 87, 88, 102, 109, 110, 113
Jennison, 109
Jennor, 99
Jeofferies, 43
Jepson, 87, 88
Jermayne, 67, 69
Jernell, 19
Jervis, 74
Jimson, 74
Joanes, 49
Joes, 43
Johnes, 12, 19, 99, 106, 111
Johnson, 14, 24, 39, 40, 42, 65, 75, 85, 99, 100, 103, 110, 111
Jones, 23, 31, 33, 34, 36, 39, 59, 74, 84, 99, 100, 103, 105, 106, 107, 108, 109, 111, 112, 113
Jope, 41
Jordan, 33
Jostlin, 20
Joyner, 103, 110
Jurden, 70

K.

Kallender, 75, 76
Keble, 88
Keele, 17
Keene, 59
Kemball, 51, 52
Kemp, 56, 106, 110
Kemper, 75
Kent, 58, 59, 70, 71, 110
Kerbie, 42, 106
Kerley, 58
Kett, 99
Kettell, 29
Key, 100, 113
Keyne, 39
Keysie, 114
Kibie, 107
Kilborne, 26, 51
Kilin, 48
Killingball, 43
Kinderslie, 105
King, 24, 35, 36, 52, 53, 56, 59, 71, 102, 105, 106, 109, 110, 113, 114
Kingsman, 70
Kingston, 112
Kirk, 25
Kirtland, 15

Knappe, 44
Knight, 39, 56, 60, 80, 99, 103, 107, 108
Knipe, 109
Knore, 34
Knowles, 25, 103, 112

L.

Lacie, 107
Lacon, 113
Ladd, 70
Lake, 103, 106, 108, 112
Lambart. 23, 47
Lamberd, 103
Lambert, 112
Lambeth, 107
Lampeugh, 99
Lampley, 109
Lamyn, 102
Lane, 77, 104, 107
Lange, 107
Langredge, 99
Lannin, 15
Large, 79
Larkyn, 109, 111
Latcome, 71
Lavere. 68
Laverick, 52
Laud, 69
Launder, 36
Lawes, 45
Lawrence, 16, 99, 104, 106, 112
Laycock, 105
Laydon, 105
Layton, 100
Lea, 18, 54
Leach, 18, 24
Leachman, 111
Leake, 33, 105, 109
Leas, 113
Leaves, 42, 65
Leay, 104
Lecht, 86
Lee, 86, 87, 100, 102, 103, 106, 107, 108, 111, 114
Leech, 102, 104
Leeds, 47
Lesten, 75
Lett, 103
Letteny, 100
Lettyne, 24
Levage, 56
Levins, 11, 101
Lewes, 40, 109
Lewis, 12, 51, 52, 84
Liddicott, 64
Lieford, 29
Lightbound, 112
Lilliot, 111
Lincoln, 45, 79, 81

Lindsey, 46
Ling, 101
Littlefield, 60
Littleball, 70
Livermore, 53
Lloyd, 42, 105, 112
Locke, 15, 102, 113
Lodge, 102
Loe, 110
Loftis, 101
Londinoys, 37
Lone, 105
Long, 32, 40, 100, 102, 103
Longsha, 106
Longwith, 105
Loomis, 27
Lord, 28
Lort, 110
Lostell, 103
Lougie, 24, 59
Love, 103
Lovell, 106
Lovley, 103
Lowe, 43, 74
Lowis, 107
Lowyun, 109
Loyd, 42
Lucocks, 103
Luddington, 19
Ludken, 45, 79, 82
Ludwell, 59
Luff, 70
Lumus, 23
Lunt, 71
Lupton, 113
Lurtray, 101
Lutterell, 106
Lyne, 38, 106
Lynley, 100, 104
Lynt, 101
Lynton, 113
Lyon, 42, 88, 100
Lysle, 87, 88

M.

Mack, 75
Mackajne, 74, 75, 76
Mackalester, 74, 75
Mackalinsten, 74
Mackally, 76
Mackane, 75
Mackannell, 74
Mackatherne, 75
Mackcunnell, 75
Mackdoel, 75
Mackdonnell, 74
Macken, 74
Mackendoche, 74
Mackenthow, 74
Macketh, 75, 76
Mackey, 74, 75, 76

INDEX OF NAMES OF PASSENGERS.

Mackfarson, 75, 76
Mackhan, 74
Mackhell, 75
Mackhollin, 75
Mackhene, 74, 76
Mackhoe, 76
Mackholme, 74
Macklude, 74
Macklyne, 75
Mackneile, 75, 76
Macknelle, 74, 75
Macknester, 74
Macknith, 75
Mackonne, 74, 75
Mackontoss, 76
Mackrose, 74
Macktentha, 76
Mackthomas, 74
Macktreth, 75, 76
Mackurnall, 75
Mackwell, 74
Mackwilliam, 74
Maddox, 15, 101
Makyn, 111
Mallion, 105
Manifold, 40
Mann, 75, 107, 112
Mannering, 11
Manning, 33, 47
Mansfield, 23, 102, 110
Manzer, 106
Mapes, 53
Marche, 58
Marcus, 87
Mare, 101
Marfutt, 99
Marritt, 113
Marrow, 100
Marrowdin, 102
Marsh, 70, 107
Marshall, 15, 34, 39, 42, 88, 106, 107
Martin, 20, 23, 35, 40, 66, 74, 104, 105-107, 114
Marvyn, 26
Mason, 20, 37, 53, 84, 105, 106, 110, 114
Masters, 101
Masterton, 86
Maston, 46
Mather, 103
Mathew, 66, 106, 110
Maudsley, 41;
Maulder, 39
Mawfrey, 108
Maxwell, 112
May, 67, 86, 107
Mayer, 81
Mayo, 109
McBrian, 106
McCoury, 106

Mecham, 103
Medgley, 112
Medley, 113
Medwell, 101
Mekins, 111
Mellison, 112
Mercer, 32, 39
Mere, 33, 34
Merrifield, 102
Merriman, 106
Merriton, 112
Merry, 66
Metcalfe, 45, 103, 111
Meverill, 109
Michell, 81
Mickell, 74 75
Mickuab, 74
Middleton, 110
Miller, 42, 75, 77, 109, 110, 114
Milleson, 74
Millett, 22
Millington, 107
Mills, 100
Milner, 39
Milward, 74, 76, 104, 107
Minterne, 68
Mitchell, 110
Mixer, 51, 52
Moier, 12
Moll, 60
Molton, 111
Moncaster, 113
Mouinges, 34
Monk, 99
Monlow, 74
Monroe, 74, 75
Montague, 69
Montgomery, 106
Montrose, 76
Monwilliam, 74, 75
Moore, 74, 81, 100
Morden, 15, 108
More, 15, 25, 26, 35, 74, 99, 100, 105, 106, 108, 110
Morecock, 30
Morfield, 81
Morgan, 109, 113
Morley, 109
Morlin, 112
Morre, 75
Morres, 58
Morrey, 43
Morris, 17, 67, 103, 109, 110
Morrish, 110
Morrison. 16, 101
Morrot, 75
Morse, 26, 56, 77
Mortagh, 102
Morton, 75, 86, 106, 107, 110
Mory, 35
Mosdell, 110

Mosse, 51
Mott, 36, 77
Moudey, 70
Moulton, 46, 47
Mountain, 102
Moyees, 102
Muckstore, 76
Mulfoot, 77
Mulleneux, 111
Mumford, 78
Munchrell, 75
Munninge, 51, 52, 77
Munson, 35, 51
Murfitt, 114
Murrill, 12
Murrin, 111
Murrow, 75, 76
Musick, 111
Muskett, 15
Mussell, 20, 106
Mussey, 70
Musslewhite, 56
Mydhouse, 102
Myles, 71
Mynnikyn, 100

N.

Nacton, 106
Naney, 24
Nash, 106
Nayler, 109
Neale, 87, 88
Neave, 48
Neaverro, 65
Necklin, 110
Nedson, 106
Negroe, 108
Nelme, 107
Nelson, 87
Nes, 88
Netbie, 107
Nettleton, 112
Nevell, 113
Newbey, 71
Newbolt, 114
Newcomb, 18, 103
Newdon, 66
Newell, 53, 54
Newman, 31, 70, 71
Newton, 113
Nichols, 23, 111
Nickerson, 45
Nicks, 100
Nishett, 100
Nisom, 100
Noble, 104, 109
Nokes, 101, 109
Norden, 113
Norman, 108
Norris, 86, 108
North, 23

Norton, 11, 71, 106
Nott, 102
Nowell, 110
Noyes, 57, 70, 71, 77
Nunn, 26
Nutbrown, 39

O.
O'Bryan, 106
Oden, 68
Offlent, 107
Offword, 100
Ogden, 101
Ogell, 102
Older, 102
Oldham, 30, 86
Olliver, 11, 50, 66
Olmstedd, 12
Olney, 16
Oneale, 76
Oneth, 67
Onge, 53
Onyon, 35
Oram, 105
Orchard, 68
Orris, 29
Osborn, 100
Osgood, 59, 70
Ossebrooke, 113
Outmore, 109
Ovell, 85
Owdie, 26
Owen, 100, 104, 111
Ownstedd, 114
Oxenbridge, 109

P.
Packer, 81
Paddey, 56
Page, 22, 44, 46, 105, 109, 114
Paine, 48, 66, 81
Pallister, 100
Palmer, 39, 51, 104, 107, 108, 110, 112
Palmerley, 23
Pancrust, 31
Panke, 114
Paple, 107
Pardy, 99
Parish, 26
Parke, 59
Parker, 23, 30, 41, 56, 59, 61, 71, 78, 108, 111
Parkinson, 106
Parler, 106
Parlin, 112
Parnell, 108
Parr, 109
Parry, 43, 109
Parryer, 15, 16
Parsons, 56, 87

Pattman, 102
Patterson, 15, 76
Patteson, 75
Paul, 108
Pautes, 87, 88
Payne, 26, 34, 108, 111
Payson, 17
Peabody, 16
Peacock, 17, 112
Peake, 19
Pearse, 65
Pease, 53, 54
Peat, 17
Peck, 80, 82, 100, 106
Pedler, 66
Peerce, 85
Peke, 105
Pell, 19, 103
Pellam, 23, 24
Pence, 99
Pendleton, 108
Pendred, 103
Penn, 107
Pennaire, 71
Pennington, 65, 110
Penny, 102
Penson, 106
Pepper, 55
Pepy, 53, 55
Perce, 26
Percy, 103
Perk, 38,
Perkins, 11, 100, 105
Perley, 16
Perry, 74, 103
Pers, 45
Persice, 68
Peter, 99
Petite, 111
Pettinger, 87
Phelps, 71, 107
Phesel, 86
Phillips, 99, 100, 106, 109, 114
Philpot, 100, 101, 106
Phinnei, 111
Phippen, 15, 104
Phipps, 113
Phylkin, 103
Picke, 65
Pickering, 87, 110
Picto, 105
Pierce, 51, 105, 112
Pike, 56, 112
Pinkley, 109
Pithouse, 56
Pittney, 21
Pitts, 81, 82, 111, 113
Place, 43, 100
Plankett, 102
Plomer, 113
Plunkett, 106

Podd, 23
Poke, 111
Pollard, 65
Pollington, 105
Pomell, 106
Poud, 60
Ponnd, 28
Ponnt, 28
Poole, 108
Poore, 61
Pope, 71, 114
Porter, 58, 100, 105, 111
Pott, 106
Potter, 26, 29, 36
Poule, 68
Powell, 105, 106, 108, 109
Poyett, 48
Pratt, 102, 112
Preston, 14, 19, 28, 43, 68, 102, 111
Price, 33, 104, 109, 113
Prichard, 99, 105, 108, 114
Priday, 106
Prier, 42
Priest, 86, 88
Prince, 77
Procter, 23, 110
Promd, 106
Prosser, 100
Pryer, 42
Pullin, 101
Punn, 75
Purefoy, 66
Purnell, 100
Purslym, 99
Puttex, 100
Pynder, 23, 110
Pynkston, 111

Q.
Querne, 75
Quicke, 68

R.
Rabey, 47
Radford, 111
Rainescroft, 113
Rainolds, 101
Rainsford, 34
Rallendra, 75
Ramsay, 110
Randall, 104
Ranse, 101
Rapan, 106
Rasbottom, 99
Rawlins, 27, 107, 112
Ray, 104
Raynne, 109
Raynor, 51, 52
Raynton, 17
Read, 39, 78, 100, 104, 107

124   INDEX OF NAMES OF PASSENGERS.

Reason, 102, 107, 108
Reddhedd, 101
Reddish, 109
Redford, 110
Redman, 105
Reed, 68
Reeves, 14, 28, 60, 77, 107
Reid, 42
Rember, 100
Rennam, 110
Reusby, 65
Reynolds, 51, 70, 88, 102, 104, 107, 108, 110
Rich, 73, 74
Richards, 12, 100, 106, 108
Richardson, 25, 77, 85, 102, 109, 110, 111, 114
Ricroft, 80, 82
Riddet, 57
Riddlesden, 23
Rider, 71
Ridley, 18, 110
Riley, 110
Ripley, 81, 82
Rishford, 102
Rising, 110
Riskymer, 104
Roaff, 58
Robards, 102
Robb, 114
Roberts, 12, 99, 103, 106, 109
Robertson, 35, 75
Robinson, 15, 35, 42, 44, 47, 74, 75, 85, 86, 99, 103, 105, 107, 113, 114
Rocks, 101
Rodes, 111
Rodgers, 78
Rods, 99
Roe, 106
Roger, 26, 39, 103, 105, 114
Roker, 105
Rolfe, 111
Rollright, 104
Rooby, 65
Rookeman, 34
Root, 33, 35, 84
Ropear, 47, 102
Rosden, 110
Rose, 42, 53, 54, 56
Roseter, 66
Ross, 74, 75, 76, 110
Rowe, 75, 102
Rowland, 110
Rowles, 111
Rowton, 25
Roye, 74
Rudge, 112
Rudglie, 106
Ruggles, 17
Rule, 112

Rum, 36
Rumball, 43
Ruosman, 68
Ruscoe, 22
Rush, 108
Russell, 20, 75, 105, 110
Rutter, 58, 106
Rymes, 100

S.

Sabyn, 114
Sadler, 58, 105
Saidwell, 105
Saiewell, 35
Saires, 108
Sakell, 111
Sall, 28
Salmon, 107, 111
Salter, 56, 68
Saltonstall, 23
Sam, 65
Samond, 28
Sampson, 30
Sanby, 99
Sanders, 58
Sandley, 108
Sanford, 113
Sangar, 58
Sankey, 24, 111
Sape, 50
Saracele, 104
Sares, 108
Saunders, 18, 66, 109
Saunderson, 111
Savage, 16, 100, 102
Savery, 70
Sawcott, 103
Sawkyn, 39
Sawter, 103
Say, 103
Sayer, 80, 84
Scarsbrick, 102
Scoates, 56
Scott, 51, 52, 75, 103, 104, 114
Scudder, 31
Sea, 99
Seabright, 113
Seager, 56
Seaver, 70
Sedden, 102
Sedgwick, 43
Seely, 106
Seere, 101
Seker, 77
Sell, 108, 110
Sellim, 27
Selman, 101
Sennod, 105
Sennott, 103
Seusion, 23
Sentence, 102

Sergeant, 101
Seriff, 100
Sessions, 103
Sessor, 75
Seward, 100
Sewell, 48
Sexton, 40
Shafflin, 56
Sharp, 13, 34, 110
Shawe, 114
Sheeres, 103
Sheering, 103
Sheicroft, 113
Shelley, 12
Shenne, 75
Shepard, 35, 36
Shepherd, 37
Sherborn, 12
Sherhack, 103
Sherin, 51
Sherlock, 111
Sherman, 51, 101
Sherwood, 53, 54
Shettleworth, 99
Shipp, 113
Shiva***, 75
Shoars, 78
Shone, 75
Shore, 113
Short, 68, 71, 108
Shuron, 75
Simes, 37
Simkins, 110
Simons, 87
Simpson, 43, 103, 110
Simson, 74, 75, 76
Sinclare, 74
Skarville, 99
Skerry, 46
Skofield, 23
Skooler, 106
Skorier, 110
Skose, 67
Skott, 51
Skouling, 80
Skyddell, 114
Skynggle, 107
Skynner, 111, 113
Slavelie, 65
Sleman, 66
Slie, 104
Smale, 56
Smallie, 11
Smallman, 102
Smart, 82, 112
Smison, 76
Smith, 18, 19, 21, 22, 24, 27, 45, 47, 51, 52, 56, 68, 76, 77, 79, 81, 82, 85, 87, 88, 99, 100, 101, 103, 104, 105, 106, 108, 109, 111, 112, 113

INDEX OF NAMES OF PASSENGERS. 125

Smitheman, 102
Smythe, 56
Snape, 111
Snathe, 103
Snignell, 112
Snow, 23, 113
Somner, 33
Sotherland, 75, 76
Southward, 114
Southworth, 87, 88
Sowthe, 99, 109
Speckman, 101
Speed, 103
Speere, 108
Spenceley, 113
Spencer, 71, 113, 114
Spendergrass, 102
Spendley, 107
Spicer, 105
Spoonard, 87
Sprall, 40
Spring, 51, 52
Sprite, 106
Spurkes, 22
Spurr, 102
Spyer, 103
Squier, 99
Stafford, 105
Stagg, 18, 19
Standy, 30
Stanford, 106
Stannion, 18
Stanley, 28, 111
Stansley, 21
Stantley, 36
Staples, 106
Stapleton, 107
Stares, 14, 84
Starr, 84
Staughton, 109
Stebing, 53, 54
Stedman, 27
Steere, 39
Steevenson, 109
Stephens, 67
Sterling, 75
Sterry, 113
Sterte, 43
Stevens, 13, 29, 36, 59, 67, 100, 109, 110, 112
Steward, 112
Stewart, 75, 76
Stiffiliynn, 110
Stiles, 14, 15
Stint, 113
Stock, 108
Stockbridge, 35
Stocker, 110
Stockton, 43
Stockwell, 108
Stoe, 107

Stokes, 42, 99, 103, 110
Stone, 20, 27, 103, 106
Stonword, 108
Stor, 103
Storey, 46
Stott, 102
Stow, 103
St. Parlin, 113
Strange, 108
Stratford, 99
Strattergood, 101
Stratton, 77
Streaton, 27
Street, 23
Streme, 43
Streter, 114
Strowde, 34
Stuebridge, 35
Studman, 19
Sturdy, 107
Sturgis, 103
Sturton, 113
Sucklin, 80
Sumes, 112
Sutton, 81, 99
Swales, 107
Swayne, 18, 20, 24, 27, 43
Sweete, 70
Sweeting, 102
Swynden, 29
Sydhe, 24
Symes, 99
Symon, 65
Symondes, 66, 101, 102, 113
Symper, 114
Syton, 78

T.

Tadde, 107
Talbot, 88
Tallcott, 12
Tarlton, 78
Tate, 105
Tatnum, 100
Tawyer, 105
Taylor, 22, 24, 29, 43, 77, 100, 105, 106, 108, 109, 112, 113
Taynter, 58
Tedder, 103
Teed, 49
Teirrer, 111
Teller, 75
Tems, 107
Tenler, 75
Terrett, 100
Terrill, 107, 114
Terry, 36, 39, 103
Thatcher, 56
Theody, 99
Thomas, 11, 42, 48, 49, 64, 65, 102, 107, 109, 110, 113

Thomlins, 25
Thomlinson, 113
Thompson, 50, 102, 109
Thomson, 29, 36, 107, 108, 111, 113
Thorne, 21, 110
Thornton, 23, 27
Thorp, 17, 104
Threlcatt, 106
Thurrogood, 114
Thurston, 48, 77
Thwaits, 19
Thwing, 25
Tibbaldes, 43
Tickens, 87
Ticknall, 42
Tilden, 82
Tiler, 75
Tilly, 31
Tingley, 19
Tisdin, 114
Tissall, 114
Titus, 17
Toller, 27
Tomkins, 43
Tomlinson, 107
Tompson, 75
Tooth, 76
Toothaker, 42
Topleife, 113
Toppan, 48
Torhe, 108
Totman, 12
Totnell, 104
Tower, 74, 79
Towne, 46, 100
Townsend, 111
Townson, 102
Trace, 70
Tracy, 86
Trane, 26
Trarice, 16, 17
Trask, 70
Tratt, 105
Travers, 70
Tredwell, 41
Tregagell, 110
Trendall, 104
Treneeghan, 65
Trentum, 40
Trenneere, 65
Trese, 107
Trewin, 65
Trigg, 100
True, 108
Trueman, 101
Truppart, 108
Trusedell, 114
Tuck, 110
Tucker, 36
Tufts, 80

INDEX OF NAMES OF PASSENGERS.

Tuke, 108
Tupper, 109
Turner, 17, 35, 72, 102, 103, 107
Turpin, 105
Tusolie, 31
Tustin, 110
Tuttell, 16, 18, 82
Twide, 78
Tybbott, 40
Tyler, 105
Tylly, 28
Tynkler, 35

U.
Ubank, 111
Uffett, 12
Underwood, 19, 46, 51
Upson, 27
Upton, 68
Usher, 99, 100
Usherwood, 113

V.
Vane, 69
Van Luecom, 114
Vardell, 110
Vassall, 35
Vassen, 56
Vaughan, 101, 111
Vem, 107
Vennable, 108
Ventimer, 106
Verren, 56
Viccars, 108
Vincent, 70, 86, 108, 110
Vynn, 102

W.
Wadd, 47
Wade, 12, 65, 102, 103, 108
Wadsworth, 12
Wakefield, 61
Walker, 105, 107, 111
Wall, 34, 109
Waller, 112
Wallis, 33, 34, 75, 103
Wallington, 59, 105
Walker, 24, 25, 49, 56, 100
Walston, 43
Walter, 50, 99, 100, 101, 112
Walton, 100, 101
Ward, 20, 50
Warerman, 66
Warner, 26
Warr, 112
Warren, 107, 108, 114
Warrener, 87
Warrington, 108
Wartumbee, 112
Washburn, 22
Wassell, 35

Waterman, 100
Watkinson, 99
Watkyns, 103
Watler, 109
Watson, 12, 102, 106, 107, 109
Wattlin, 53
Watton, 109
Watts, 101, 102, 106, 107, [112, 113
Waugh, 77
Wazzell, 105
Weatherhead, 77
Weaver, 16, 17
Webb, 56, 65, 78, 103, 104,
Webster, 111, 113 [111, 114
Weeden, 23
Weekes, 42, 67, 112
Wellman, 100, 110
Wells, 18, 23, 24, 99, 108, 110
Wellyn, 100
Welsh, 20, 114
Wendever, 107
Wentworth, 109
West, 34, 42, 70, 109, 110
West Garrett, 111
Westgarth, 102
Weston, 29, 102, 106, 113, 114
Westwood, 53, 54, 103
Weyer, 100
Wharton, 108
Whealer, 55, 59, 110
Wheat, 22
Whetston, 11, 104
Wheyler, 70
White, 12, 14, 26, 27, 30, 33, 53, 68, 70, 86, 87, 88, 99, 102, 106, 109, 112
Whiteman, 31
Whitehedd, 100, 105, 110, 113
Whitlock, 102
Whitman, 43
Whitney, 23
Whittemore, 17, 67
Whitteredd, 21
Whittington, 64
Whittle, 58
Whitton, 29, 30
Wigin, 77
Wilby, 23
Wilcocks, 108
Wilcockson, 16
Wild, 21
Wilder, 59
Wilkins, 87
Wilkinson, 28, 105, 112
Wilks, 100
Willard, 109
Wille, 67
Willet, 12
Williams, 36, 45, 47, 66, 88, 100, 102, 105, 106, 107, 108, 109, 110, 112, 113

Williamson, 16, 39, 42, 108
Willis, 102, 106
Wills, 103
Wilson, 74, 76, 87, 104, 108
Winslow, 11, 86
Winthrop, 38
Winche, 54
Winchell, 20
Winchester, 18
Wing, 53
Winke, 105
Wise, 68
Witchfield, 12
Wite, 110
With, 42
Witherell, 83
Withie, 42
Wolhouston, 18
Wolton, 114
Wood, 26, 27, 31, 37, 42, 88, 106, 107, 108, 112
Woodall, 76
Woodbridge, 70
Woodcock, 110
Woodcott, 108
Woodell, 74
Wooden, 68
Woodford, 11
Woodgreene, 108
Woodstock, 107
Woodman, 36, 55
Woodward, 17, 20, 51, 52
Worden, 27
Worrall, 110
Worster, 77
Wrast, 16
Wreuch, 112
Wright, 44, 82, 109, 110
Write, 103, 106
Writt, 66
Wurfris, 57
Wy, 103
Wvlde, 30
Wylie, 29
Wynd, 100, 112
Wyndell, 27
Wyndibank, 69
Wynkles, 102
Wynstonly, 105
Wynter, 112

Y.
Yates, 34, 101, 109
Yatman, 106, 111
Yeomans, 100
Yonge, 49
York, 112
Yott, 111
Young, 101, 105, 106, 109
Younglove, 42

INDEX OF PERSONS,

PRINCIPALLY OF THOSE CONNECTED IN SOME WAY WITH THE EMIGRANT FOUNDERS.

NOTE.—Those names to which Mr. is added denotes that they were Masters of Emigrant Ships.

A.
Abbot, George, 69
Acklin, John, Mr. 102
Andrews, William, Mr. 44, 51
Apiano, P. 110
Arundel, Earl of, 90
Ashley, ——, Mr. 41
Athridge, Count of, 96
Austin, John, 83, 84

B.
Babb, Thomas, Mr. 41, 72
Bancks, Caleb, 83
Banks, William, 101
Barrel, Robert, 83
Barrow, Giles, 76
Batten, Robert, Mr. 60
Baynard, Thomas, 97
Beadley, John, 76
Beex, John, 73, 74
Bellingham, Richard, 77
Bendall, Freegrace, 78
Bertie, Robert, 69
Billinge, Cornelius, Mr. 104
Bindon, Viscount, 98
Blackler, Peter, Mr. 112
Boole, Joseph, 66
Bostock, Edward, Mr. 32, 38
Bostock, Thomas, Mr. 36, 37, 38
Boswell, Edward, Mr. 33
Boys, William, 82
Bradley, John, 76
Brookehaven, Jo. Mr. 104
Browne, Philip, 51, 55
Bundocke, William, Mr. 15, 17
Burche, ——, Mr. 105
Burnney, William, 78

C.
Carlisle, Earl of, 107
Cary, ——, 97

Champante, Henry, 59, 61
Charles I., 17, 89
Chute, Edmond, 83
Clere, Thomas, 51, 55
Clynton, William, De, 96
Cobham, Reignold De, 96
Coke, John, Sir, 90
Colepeper, William, 83
Cooper, Robert, Mr. 20, 22, 24, 28, 29, 30
Cooper, William, Mr. 27, 55, 57
Cordell, Robert, 24
Cosengton, Stephen, 96
Cottington, Lord, 69, 90
Cotton, John, 72
Coventry, Thomas, Sir, 69, 90
Cowper, Robert. See Cooper.
Cranfield, Lord, 98
Crispe, Han. 83
Cromwell, Oliver, 72
Cutting, John, Mr. 53, 54, 55

D.
Dayrell, Marmaduke, Sir, 97
Denison, Doctor, 72
Dennis, Robert, Mr. 103
Dingley, N. 57, 59, 61
Dorset, Earl of, 90
Downes, George, Mr. 111
Drake, Francis, Sir, 9
Duke, Edward, 83

E.
Edmonds, Thomas, Sir, 90
Elizabeth, Queen, 98
English, John, 96
Epitaphs, 98
Erskine, Thomas, 69

F.
Fane, Henry, Sir. See Vane.

Farronds, R. 19
Fenn, Alderman, 19
Fleeges, John, 96
Flower, John, Mr. 110
Foxcroft, George, 63
Froiden, Franc, 83

G.
Gardner, Thomas, 83, 84
Gee, John, 82, 83, 84
Genealogy, Origin of, 7
Gibbs, Jo:, Mr. 42
Gilbert, Humphrey, Sir, 10
Godfrey, Thomas, 84
Goodladd, Richard, Mr. 107
Googe, William, Mr. 48
Gorges, Ferdinando, Sir, 89, 93, 95-97
Gursham, Robert, 84
Gourney, William, 67
Greene, John, Mr. 73, 74, 76
Greene, William, 73. 74
Grenfield, Thomas, 96
Grimes, Gilbert, Mr. 105
Grimston, ——. 101
Guyse, John, 74

H.
Hankford, R. Sir, 96
Harding, William, 96
Hardres, ——. 37
Harman, Thomas, Mr. 84, 101-2
Hackwell, R. Mr. 28, 31-3, 35
Hatch, John, 96
Hayes, Edmund, 83, 84
Hill, Henry, 50
Hodges, Jo., Mr. 19, 20
Hondius Judocus, 10
Honnywood, John, 84
Hopson, John, Mr. 68

INDEX OF PERSONS.

Howard, John, Sir, 96
Howard, Lord, 97
Hubbard, William, 89
Hyones, ——, 97

I.
Irish, Thomas, Mr. 103, 113

J.
Jackson, Thomas, 84
James I. 9, 90
Jay, Thomas, Sir, 15
Jermyn, Thomas, Sir, 69
Jobson, John, Mr. 57

K.
Kelly, Earl of, 69
Kemble, Thomas, 73, 76
Kinnersley, Edward, 97
Knapp, John, 57
Knowler, John, 84

L.
Lancaster, Earl of, 96
Langram, Rowland, Mr. 109
Laud, William, 69, 89
Lea, Robert, Mr. 20, 24–6
Leeth, Joseph, 84
Leicster, Jo:, Mr. 34, 40
Lincoln, Earl of, 96, 98
Lincoln, Solomon, 78
Lock, Robert, Mr. 77
Londinoys, Richard, 37
Lovell, William, 96
Lunt, George, 68
Luttrell, ——, 97

M.
Macaulay, Lord, 8
Manchester, Earl of, 69, 90
Mann, Edward, 51, 55
Marshall, Samuel, 83
Martin, John, Mr. 81
Martin, Thomas, 33
Mason, Captain, 12
May, Jo:, Mr. 31, 39
Mayhew, Thomas, 44, 50
Meantys, John, 70
Mildmaye, Henry, Sir, 33
Montagne, Henry, 69
Moore, John, 97
More, Thomas, Sir, 98

Morris, John, 76
Marsh, Gabriel, 70
Morton, Thomas, 96
Murphy, Henry C., 85
Muskett, Simon, 15

N.
Newton, ——, 96, 97
Nicholls, Edward, 84
Nicolas, Nicholas Harris, Sir, 8
Norfolk, Duke of, 96, 97
Northampton, Marquess of, 96
Nottock, John, 73, 74

O.
Ouldhall, Edmund, Sir, 96
Ouldhall, William, Sir, 96

P.
Payne, Edward, Mr. 23, 25, 29
Pearce, ——, Mr. 31, 32
Pedigrees, Origin of, 7; of Harlakenden, 37; of Gorges, 96, 97
Pelling, Edward, 76, 77
Phillips, John, 84
Philpott, John, 77
Portland, Earl of, 90
Pownall, Thomas, 89
Poynts, Anthony, Sir, 96, 97

R.
Ranton. See Raynton.
Rawson, Edward, 73, 74, 76
Raynton, Nicholas, Sir, 17, 24
Rich, Charles, 73, 74
Rich, Robert, 73, 74, 76
Richardson, C. B., 85
Roberts, Lewis, 10
Robinson, John, 85, 88
Romsey, James, Mr. 99
Russell, Theobald, Sir, 96

S.
Samsbury, W. N., 50
Sandford, William, 84
Sheppard, Justice, 101
Sidney, Robert, Sir, 98
Smith, John, 9, 10
Smith, Thomas, 19
Somerby, H. G., 71, 86, 99
Southcott, Edward, Sir, 97

Speake, George, Sir, 97
Spencer, Edmund, 98
Spencer, Edward, Sir, 88
Spencer, James, 97
Sprague, Richard, Mr. 78
Stace, Fregift, 83, 84
Stagg, William, Mr. 18, 19, 21, 22, 24–6
Stephens, Thomas, 97
Swinnok, Thomas, 83
Syres, Robert, 70, 71

T.
Thoroughgood, ——, Mr. 68
Thorp, J., 17
Thurston, William, 84
Trarice, Nicholas, Mr. 15–17, 20
Trenchard, ——, 97

V.
Vane, Henry, Sir, 69, 90

W.
Walsh, John, Sir, 97
Warren, Thomas, 83, 84
Waymoth, James, Mr. 111
Wenb, ——, 97
Webb, Thomas, Mr. 41
Whitcomb, John, 21
White, John, Mr. 14
White, Roger, 88
White, Rowland, 98
Whitehouse, Thomas, 71
Whitmor, William, Sir, 24
Whitor, George, Sir, 17, 38
Whitmore, W. H., 85
William the Conqueror, 6
Willis, ——, 93
Willoughby, Lord, 69, 96
Witherley, John, Mr. 82
Wood, Elias, 83
Wood, Thomas, Mr. 100
Worthy, James, 68
Wren, Christopher, Sir, 14
Wurfries, Thomas, 57, 59, 61
Wyndebank, Francis, Sir, 69, 90

Y.
York, Archbishop of, 90
Young, Joseph, Mr. 40

INDEX OF PLACES.

A.
Akecitron, 17
Albion, 9
Allsaints, 32
Allsaints Staynings, 22
Amesbury, 56
Arkston, 17
Auckstrey, 17
Ashberton, 67
Ashford, 83, 84
Ashmore, 58
Attleborough, 81
Auckstrey, 17
Augmentation Office, 9
Austerfield, 86
Aylesford, 83

B.
Baddow, 33
Bampton, 67
Barbadoes, 89, 99–104–14
Barnstable, 67, 68
Barrow, 80
Basing, 60
Batcombe, 97
Benenden, 30
Bermudas, 108, 110
Billerecay, 22
Bishopstoke, 60
Blackwell Hall, 19
Blechindon, 37
Bodmin, 65
Boston, 45, 46, 73, 77
Bradish, 50
Brampton, 48
Branford, 38
Brencesley, 56
British Museum, 7–9
Brixam, 68
Bury, 87

C.
Caen, 87
Callis, 96
Cambridge, 81
Canterbury, 84–6
Cardinham, 66
Carlton, 48
Carlton Ride, 12
Carlton.Rod, 48
Caversham, 56
Chapter House, 9
Charington, 85
Charlestown, 45
Chelsea, 98
Chetsum, 86
Chidleigh, 65
Clovelly, 97
Colchester, 87
Corke, 65
Craiebrook, 32
Crediton, 66
Croconpill, 62
Cullorne, 97

D.
Dartmouth, 67
Devyses, 56
Doctors Commons, 8
Dornick, 45
Downton, 56
Dover, 84, 85
Duffield, 17
Dunbar, battle, 72
Dunhead, 58
Dunstable, 32

E.
Eastwell, 84, 85
Eaton Bray, 32
Edge Hill, 69
Ell-Tisley, 17
Elzing, 49
Evesham, 22
Exerdeu, 40
Exeter, 64, 66, 67, 98
Exminster, 68
Exon, 64, 66–8

F.
Faversham, 84, 85
Fenchurch, 57
Florida, 10

G.
Genealogy, Science of, 7

Gonsham, 56, 59
Gravesend, 76–8, 102, 108
Great Chart, 84
Great Comberton, 48
Great Dalby, 65
Great Ellingham, 81
Great Killingham, 44
Great Torrington, 67
Great Yarmouth, 46–7
Guindiron, 65

H.
Hampsworth, 56
Hampton, 55, 60
Harpley(?) Hall, 81
Hawkhurst, 20
Hedcorn, 84
Helston, 65, 66
Henley, 59
Hernhill, 33
Hevitree, 98
Hingham, 78, 79
Hinxell, 83
Holborne, 101
Holston, 65, 66
Honiton, 67
Horrell, 59, 60
Horsington, 96

I.
Ipswich, 44, 51–6, 81, 87
Island of Providence, 104
Isle of Wight, 68
Isleworth, 31

J.
Jacobstow, 66

K.
Keniton Magna, 58
Kingston upon Thames, 19

L.
Lanceston, 65
Langford, 56, 58
Launden, 15
Leicester, 86
Leyden, 85

INDEX OF PLACES.

Lincoln, 64
Little Minories, 31
London. 8, 56, 61, 65, 67, 68, 84, 86–8, 99
Long Sutton, 58
Louisiana, 10
Ludswan, 66
Luggom, 66
Luxulian, 65
Lyme, 68

M.
Maidstone, 83
Marrozun, 66
Maymard [Mynhead], 67
Melchitt Parke, 58
Milford, 55
Modbury, 68
Moncksoon, 86
Monteratt, 65
Moortel, 87

N.
Nazing, 17
New Albion, 9
New Buckingham, 47
Newbury, 69, 86
New England, origin of name, 9; Maps of, 10; Laud's Commission for governing, 89; Gorges' Commission as Governor of, 93
New France, 10
Newton Abbot, 67
Northborne, 84
Northill, 65
Northton, 33
Northwich, 44-6, 48-50, 86, 88
Novascotia, 10

O.
Ormsby, 46, 47

P.
Paranenth, 65
Pedigrees, Origin of, 7
Penryn, 65
Penton, 57, 58
Peter Tavey, 65
Platford, 56
Plimpton, 65

Plymouth, 64, 67
Portsmouth, 71
Prerogative Court, 7
Providence (Island of,) 104

Q.
Quakers, 77

R.
Reading, 55
Remembrancers' Office, 9
Rochester, 87
Rolls Chapel, 9, 11, 43
Romsey, 56, 59
Rye, 44

S.
St. Albans, 16
St. Alphage, Cripplegate, 19
St. Brage, 65, 66
St. Buttolphs, 17
St. Catherins, 102
St. Christophers, 64, 66-7, 99-104
St. Cullum, 64, 66
St. Giles Cripplegate, 14, 41
St. Gilt, 65
St. Hillary, 66
St. Ives, 65
St. Katherins, 17, 105
St. Lawrence, 31
St. Margarets, 49
St. Mildreds, 14
St. Olives, 37
St. Saviors, 22
St. Stephens, 65, 67
St. Thomas the Apostle, 68
St. Tiffey, 64
St. Tue, 66
St. Vivian, 66
Salem, 48, 49
Salisbury, 56, 60
Sandwich, 82, 83–6
Sarum, 56, 60, 87
Scotch Prisoners, 72, 73
Scrooby, 87
Semley, 58
Shaftsbury, 58
Sherington, 15
Shiplake, 59
Skratley, 46

Somer Islands, 108
Southampton, 55, 57, 59, 60, 71
Southold, 50
Stanstede Abbey, 17
Staple, 85
State Paper Office, 9
Stepney, 15, 33, 35, 36
Stoke Cannon, 68
Stoke Gabriel, 67
Stoke Pomeroy, 68
Stonehouse, 65
Sudbury, 21
Sutton Mandeville, 57
Symon Ward, 65

T.
Tenterden, 82–4
Thisselworth, 31
Tottnes, 65
Towcester, 32
Tower of London, 9, 105
Truro, 65

U.
Upton Gray, 58

V.
Virginia, 68, 72, 89

W.
Wallen Lizard, 66
Wantage, 66
Wapping, 25
Warhorn, 37
Washboro, 66
Washford, 67
Westminster, 93
Wincklye, 65
Windham, 79, 81
Withiell, 66
Witzbuts, 86
Wollerbe [Worlaby], 50
Wrottwell, 50
Wraxall, 97
Wrentham, 48, 86
Wrington, 86

Y.
Yarmouth, 44, 47-50, 87
Yealing, 56
York, 86

INDEX OF THE SHIPS

WHICH BROUGHT EMIGRANTS TO NEW ENGLAND, &c.

A.
Abigail, 28, 31–8
Alexander, 105
Amity, 111
Ann and Elizabeth, 104
Arabella, 78

B.
Batcheler, 41
Bevis, 60
Blessing, 34, 40

C.
Christian, 14
Clement and Job, 69
Confidence, 57, 60

D.
Defence, 32, 36–9
Desire, 31, 33, 63
Diligent, 81
Dorset, 110

E.
Elizabeth, 18, 19, 21, 24–6, 55
Elizabeth Anne, 20, 22, 24
Elizabeth Bonadventure, 69
Elizabeth and Dorcas, 69
Encrease. See Increase.
Expectation, 104

F.
Faulcon de London, 103, 113
Fellowship, 63
Frances, 55

H.
Hercules, 69, 71, 82
Hopewell, 15, 17, 19, 41, 71, 72, 100

I.
Increase, 20, 22, 24–6

J.
James, 31, 39, 55, 57
John and Sarah, 73, 74, 76
John of London, 111

L.
Love, 40

M.
Margaret, 66
Mary Anne, 48
Mary and John, 68–70
Mathew, 107

N.
Neptune, 61, 62, 69

P.
Paul of London, 102
Peter Bonaventure, 101–2
Pide Cow, 38, 41
Planter, 15–21, 69

R.
Rebecca, 20
Reformation, 69
Robert Bonaventure, 64
Rose, 44

S.
Sea Flower, 69
Speedwell, 77
Suzan and Ellin, 23, 25, 29

T.
Truelove, 42, 69

U.
Unity, 68

W.
William and Francis, 11
William and George, 64
William and John, 109

CATALOGUE OF BOOKS

FOR SALE AT THE OFFICE OF THE REGISTER,

17 TREMONT ST. (UP STAIRS) BOSTON.

☞ Authors and Publishers of TOWN or LOCAL HISTORIES, GENEALOGIES, &c. will find it to their interest to send a few copies to the Publisher, for sale.

HISTORIES, ETC.

Addison Co., Vt., Hist. of, by Saml. Swift,	50
Ancient and Honorable Artillery Company, Hist. of, 1st *edition*,	1 00
Agawam, Simple Cobbler of, by Ward,	50
Andover, History of, by Abbot,	1 00
Attleborough, History of, by Daggett,	75
Bailey's Dictionary, *folio*,	3 50
" Journal and Mem., by Bartlet, 8vo	1 25
Barnstable, Palfrey's Centen. at, *paper*,	25
Belknap's American Biography. 2 vols.	3 00
Berkshire Jubilee, Hist. of, 1844,	75
Boston, Drake's Hist. of, r. 8vo. *half Turkey*,	5 00
" " " " *half calf*,	5 00
" " " " *cloth*,	4 50
" Eng., Thompson's Hist. of,	9 50
" Second Church. Hist. of by Robbins,	1 50
" Brattle Street Church, Hist. of, by S. K. Lothrop,	75
" Orators, Hundred, by J. S. Loring,	2 50
" Quincy's Municipal Hist. of,	1 25
" East, Hist. of, by W. H. Sumner,	3 50
Belchertown, Hist. Sketch of Churches in, by Doolittle,	75
Beverly, Hist of, by Stone,	1 25
Berkshire Co., Hist. of.	1 25
Bridgewater, Hist. of, by Mitchell,	2 00
Cambridge Epitaphs, by Harris,	1 00
Connecticut Hist. Coll., by J. W. Barber,	2 50
Clap, (Roger,) Memoirs of, 12mo.	38
Chronology of Paper and Paper Making, by J. Munsell, (*paper*.)	1 00
Candia, N. H., F. B. Eaton, 8vo.	50
Concord. N. H., by N. Bouton,	3 00
Crosby's Annual Obituary Notices, 2 vols.,	4 00
Camden, Hist. of, by J. L. Locke,	1 00
Charlestown, First Church, Hist. of, by Budington,	1 50
Charlemont as a Plantation, by J. White, containing Historical Disc., &c.	38
Concord, Shattuck's Hist of,	2 50
" Centennial, by Bouton,	50
Cushman Celebration, Proceed. at, in 1855,	25
" Monument, Consecra. of, in 1858,	40
Danvers Centennial Celebration, 8vo. *plates*,	1 00
Davenport, Iowa, Hist. of, by Wilkie.	1 00
Dedham, Mann's Annals of,	1 00
" Pulpit, 8vo., *scarce*,	1 50
Dodd's Revolutionary Memorials,	50
Dorchester, Hist. of, *cloth*,	2 50
" Blake's Annals of, 12mo.	38
" Everett's Address, July 4, 1855,	50
Drake, Daniel, Memoir of, by Mansfield,	75
Drake's Book of the Indians, 8vo., *cloth*,	1 50
Dunstable, Hist. of, by C. J. Fox, *scarce*,	1 50
Duxbury, Winsor's Hist. of, 8vo.	1 75
Eastham, History of, by Enoch Pratt,	1 25
Ecclesiastical Hist. of N. Eng., Felt's, 8vo.	2 50
Essex Memorial, by Newhall, *scarce*,	75
" Institute, Coll. of, 5 Nos., *each*,	25
Framingham, Barry's Hist. of,	1 50
Forest Hills Cemetery, Hist. of,	1 00
Farmer's Gen. Register,	5 00
Gardiner and Pittston, Hanson's Hist. of,	1 00
Gilmanton, Hist. of, by Lancaster,	1 50
Gloucester, by John Babson, 8vo., pp. 610,	2 50
Groton, Butler's Hist. of,	3 00
Hadley, Bi-Centennial at, 1859,	25
Hanover, Hist. of, J. S. Barry, 8vo.	2 00
Hampton, N. H., Dow's Centennial Disc.,	25
Harwinton, Chipman's Hist. of, *cloth*,	1 25
" " " *paper*,	1 00
Hampden Pulpit, 12mo., 1854,	50
Henry's Sketches of Moravian Life, 12mo. *cloth*,	1 00
Hunter's Founders of New Plymouth, London, 1854, 8vo.	2 00
Hinman's Conn. Settlers, Nos. 1 to 5 inclusive,	2 50
Hinman's Antiquities,	1 00
Historical Magazine, 3 vols. *each*,	2 50
Hopkinton, Howe's Cent. Dis. at,	25
Indian Captivities,	75
Ipswich, History of, by J. B. Felt, with portrait, and *Index*,	1 75
Johnson's Pastors and Ch. of Washington,	75
Kentucky, Hist. Sketches of, by L. Collins,	2 50
Lamb, Gen. John, Life and Times, by Leake,	1 50

Landing at Cape Anne, with Historical Documents by J. W. Thornton, 1 00
Leicester, Hist. of, by Washburn, 2 00
Leominster, History of, by D. Wilder, 75
Lee, Hist of, by A. Gale, 25
Litchfield, History of, by Kilbourne, 1 50
Long Island, Thompson's Hist. of, 1st ed. 1 50
Magnalia, Mather's, 2 vols. 4 00
Malden, Hist. of, by McClure, 12mo. 75
" Dedication at, *paper*, 25
Manchester, N. H., Potter's Hist. of, 2 50
Massachusetts, Young's Chronicles of, 1 50
" Hist. of Western, by Holland, 2 vols. 2 50
" Currency, by J. B. Felt, 1 50
Maine, by Williamson, 2 vols. 5 00
" Ancient Dominions of, by Sewall, 2 00
Maine Hist. Soc. Coll., II. III. IV., each 1 50
Marlboro', Hist. of First Ch. in, by A. Field, 50
Marshfield, Mem. of, by M. A. Thomas, 38
Mason, N. H., History of, by J. B. Hill, 1 75
Mason, N. H., with Memoir of Rev. E. Hill, 2 00
Massachusetts, Young's Chronicles of, 1 50
Mendon Association, Hist. of, by Rev. M. Blake, 12mo. 75
Michigan, Hist. of, by E. M. Sheldon, 1 00
Memoirs of an Amer. Lady, by Mrs. Grant, 75
Merrimack Valley, Researches in, Hist. and Gen., by A. Poor, Nos. 1 & 2, p. 300, 2 00
Middleborough, Church Members, 8vo. 25
Middlebury, Vt., Hist. of by Saml. Swift, with a Hist. of the County, 2 00
Moravian Monuments, 8vo, *cloth*, 1 00
Natick, History of, by O. N. Bacon, 8vo. 1 50
" " by Biglow, 50
New Bedford, History of, by D. Ricketson, 12mo. 1 25
New England Chronology, by T. Prince, *illustrated with portraits*, 5 00
New England, History of, by Hubbard. Notes by Harris. *Plates*. 3 50
New England Churches, vindicated, by Wise, *reprint*, 75
New England Savage's Gen. Dictionary, 2 vols, *cloth*, 6 00
New England, Winthrop's Journal, by Savage, 2 vols. 4 00
News from New England respecting Indian War of 1675, small 4to., *neat*, 50
New Hampshire Churches, Hist. of, 8vo. 1 50
" " as it is, by E. A. Charlton, 1 50
New London, Caulkins's Hist. of, 3 00
Newbury, Hist. of, by J. Coffin, 1 50
Newton, History of, by Jackson, 1 50
New England's Memorial, &c. (Reprint by Congregational Board.) 2 00
New York, Western, Hotchkin's Hist. of, 1 50
" by Denton, 1685, 75
" City, Hist. of, by M. L. Booth, 3 50
Northampton, Hist. Sketch by S. Williams, 1815, 25

Norton, Clark's Hist. of, 1 75
Nova Scotia, by T. C. Haliburton, 2 vols. 3 00
Newberry, (S.C.) Annals of, by J. O'Neall, 1 25
Norwich, Ct., Hist. Address by D. C. Gilman, 1 00
Norwich Jubilee (The), pp. 304, *half calf.* 1 50
" " *cloth*, 1 25
" " *paper*, 1 00
N. H. Colls., Farmer & Moore's, 3 vols. 7 00
Norfolk, (Va.) Hist of, 1 50
Norfolk, (Conn.) Hist. of, by Roys, 75
Onondago Co., N. Y., by Clark, 2 vols. 4 00
Penhallow's Indian Wars, 4to., *reprint*, 1 50
Plumer, Gov. Wm., Memoir of, by A. P. Peabody, 1 50
Portland, History of, Part 2, by Willis, 1 00
Pittsburgh, History of, by Craig, 75
Pennsylvania and West New Jersey, by Gabriel Thomas, 1698, 12mo. Facsimile edition, 1 50
Pilgrim Memorial, by Russell, 88
Plummer Hall, Salem, proceedings at dedication of, 1857, 38
Plymouth, Pilgrim Celebration, 1853, 1 00
" Memorial, by W. S. Russell, *greatly improved edition* 12mo. *Many plates, cloth, gilt*, 1 00
Pittsfield, by D. D. Field, 38
Rehoboth, Hist. of, by Bliss, 1836, 1 00
Remarkable Providences, by Increase Mather, London, 1856. *A reprint of the edition of* 1684, 1 25
Rowley, History of, by Gage, 1 88
Roxbury, Hist. of, by C. M. Ellis, 1 00
" Grammar School in, Hist. of, by Dillaway, 88
Salisbury, Vt., Hist. of, by Weeks, 1 25
Sabine's Centennial Address, 38
Salem, Annals of, by Felt, 2 vols. 4 00
San Francisco, Hist. of, by Soulé, &c. 2 00
Shaw, Wm. S., Memorials of, by J. B. Felt, 75
Shrewsbury, Ward's Hist. of, 8vo. 2 00
South Boston, Hist. of, by Simonds, 1 00
Stockbridge, Jones's Hist. of, 1 00
Suffield, Ct., 150th an. of Death of Rev. B. Ruggles, 1859, 50
Temple, N. H., Hist. of, by H. A. Blood, 2 00
Templeton Centennial, by Adams, 1857, 50
Thomas's Reminiscences, 2 vols., 2 50
Tymms's Topography of the Counties of England, 7 vols. 7 00
Taunton, Emery's Hist. Min., 2 vols. 2 00
Thanksgiving Proclamations by Continental Cong. and Govs. of several states 2 00
Union, Me., Hist of, by Sibley, 1 50
Watertown, Bond's Genealogies, &c. 4 00
Watson's Men and Times of the Revolution, 1 25
Waterbury, (Conn.) by H. Bronson, 2 50
Warren, (R. I.) Hist. of, 18mo. 62
" (Me.) Eaton's Hist. of, 12mo. *map* 1 75

West Chester, by Robt. Bolton, 2 vols.	3 50
Whately, Hist. of, by J. H. Temple,	38
Woodbury, (Conn.,) Cothren's Hist. of,	2 50
" " Bi-Centennial of, 1859,	75
Wellington's Half Century Sermon, Templeton, 1857,	25
Windsor, Ct., by H. R. Stiles,	5 00
Westminster, 100th An. of incorporation, 1859,	50
Wisconsin, Lapham's,	75
Worthington, Hist. of, by Rice,	75

GENEALOGIES.

Abbott, by A. and E. Abbott,	1 50
Blake, by Samuel Blake,	1 00
Brainard, by D. D. Field,	1 50
Brigham, by Abner Morse,	1 50
Chapman, by F. W. Chapman,	3 00
Chauncy Memorial, by W. C. Fowler,	3 50
Connecticut Families, by N. Goodwin,	2 00
Cushman, by H. W. Cushman,	3 00
Davenport, by A. B. Davenport,	2 50
Day, by G. E. Day, (in paper,)	1 00
Dudley, by Dean Dudley, " "	1 50
Eliot, by W. H. Eliot, Jr., and W. S. Porter,	1 00
Flint, by J. Flint and J. H. Stone,	1 25
Goddard, by W. A. Goddard,	75
Haven, by Josiah Adams,	50
Herrick, by Jedediah Herrick, 8vo. *cloth*,	1 25
Hodges, by A. D. Hodges,	25
Hoyt, by D. W. Hoyt,	1 50
Judd, by S. Judd,	62
Leland, by S. Leland,	3 00
Locke, by J. G. Locke,	3 00
Lawrence, by John Lawrence,	1 50
Leverett, by C. E. Leverett, 8vo., *cloth*,	1 50
Moody, by C. C. P. Moody,	40
Nash, by S. Nash, 8vo.	1 25
Prentice, by C. J. F. Binney,	2 00
Rawson, by S. S. Rawson,	1 00
Rice, by A. H. Ward,	2 00
Scranton, by E. Scranton, 8vo.	50
Shattuck, by L. Shattuck,	2 50
Sill, by George G. Sill,	1 00
Steele, by D. S. Durrie, (*in paper*,)	2 00
Stetson, by J S. Barry, 12mo.	50
Stiles, by H. R. Stiles, 8vo , *paper*,	25
Thayer, and thirteen other families,	1 50
Tainter History, by Dean W. Tainter,	1 25
Taintor Family, by C. M. Taintor,	38
Turner, by J. Turner,	75
Vinton Family,	3 00
" " Genealogy of, abridged, with allied Families,	2 00
Worcester, by J. F. Worcester,	1 00
Woodman, by Joshua Coffin,	25
Ward, by A. H. Ward, 8vo.	2 00
Willard, by J. Willard,	3 00
Wight, by D. P. Wight,	75
White, by A. S. Kellogg,	2 50

RARE ENGLISH BOOKS

LATELY SELECTED IN ENGLAND

AND NOW OFFERED

AT VERY LOW PRICES,

AT No. 17 TREMONT STREET, (Up Stairs,) . . . . . . BOSTON.

THE LONDON MAGAZINE, from its commencement, in 1732, to 1779—wanting volumes for 1767, 1768, 1773, 1775, and 1778—in all, 44 volumes. Continuous from 1 to 35, inclusive. From 1 to 24, bound uniformly. *Few plates deficient in some of the later volumes.* $20.00

    This work was a rival of the Gentleman's Magazine, and was conducted in a spirit more liberal than that work. It is peculiarly rich in matters relating to America. All the details of the old French and Indian wars are much more full than in any other work, and the events are illustrated by maps, charts, and views, well engraved.

BRADY'S INTRODUCTION TO OLD ENGLISH HISTORY, &c. Folio. London: 1686. 3.00

    Contains a vast number of the ancient Norman names of those who came in with the Conqueror, from Doomsday and other authentic sources.

BAILEY'S DICTIONARIUM BRITANNICUM: Or a more compleat Universal Etymological Dictionary than any extant. . . . . 2d edition. London: 1736. Folio. *Old binding, but good copy of the best edition.* 3.00

    A work to which Johnson and subsequent lexicographers have been more indebted than they ever acknowledged.

    ☞ No student should be without Bailey.

LODGE'S (Edmund) LIFE OF SIR JULIUS CÆSAR, Knight, Judge of the High Court of Admiralty, &c., during the Reign of Queen Elizabeth, &c. With 18 exquisitely engraved portraits. London: 1827. Royal 4to. *Uncut.* 2.50

HONDIUS (Judocus) HISTORIA MUNDI: or Mercator's Atlas. Containing his Cosmographical Description of the Fabricke and Figure of the World. Lately rectified in divers places, as also beautified and enlarged with new Mappes and Tables. Englished by W. Saltonstall. London: 1635. Folio. 3.50

    A very thick volume of upwards of 1000 pages, with numerous maps, including several of America and its islands.

CAMDEN'S REIGN OF ELIZABETH, written at the request of Lord Burlegh. 4th edition. London: 1688. Folio. *Old calf.* 3.00

Contains a fine portrait of Elizabeth. The work is of the utmost importance to the student of English history, inasmuch as Camden was an eye witness to many of the thrilling events he describes.

THE WORKS OF ABRAHAM COWLEY. 7th edition. London: 1681. Folio. *Fine, bright copy, in calf, gilt—splendid portrait by Faithorn.*

THE BIBLE according to the version of Munster, and New Testament by Erasmus (in Latin). 1539. 8vo. *Fine condition.* 2.00

ANBURY, Thomas, Travels through the Interior Parts of America. In a series of Letters. By an Officer. London: 1789. In 2 vols. 8vo. *Good copy of a rare work.* 6.00

The author was an officer in Burgoyne's army, and was taken prisoner by the Americans when that wing of the British army fell into their hands. A graphic and thrilling personal narrative.

BAILEY, Nathan. M. J. Justini ex Trogi Pompeii Histories Externis. Libri XLIV..... To which is added, the words of JUSTIN, disposed in a grammatical or natural order, in one column, so as to answer, as near as can be, word for word to an English version, as literal as possible in the other..... London: 1732. 8vo. *New, half calf.* 1.50

A valuable classic, edited by the learned Bailey, the author of the famous Dictionary.

BAILEY, Nathan. All the Familiar Colloquies of Desiderius Erasmus, concerning Men, Manners, and Things. Translated into English. 2d edition. London: 1733. *A fine copy, in full calf, of* GREAT ERASMUS.

BROWNE, Thomas..... Historie of the Life and Reigne of that Famous Princesse Elizabeth..... London: 1629. 4to. *Newly bound, full green Turkey.* 2.50

Curious portrait of Elizabeth on reverse of title.

CLARKE, Samuel. The Life and Death of Alexander the Great, the first Founder of the Grecian Empire..... As also the Life and Death of Charlemagne, the first Founder of the French Empire. London: 1665. 4to. *Half Morocco.* 1.00

The well-known and voluminous author of "A Looking-glass for Saints and Sinners."

BURNEY, James, Capt., F. R. S. A Chronological History of Northeastern Voyages of Discovery..... London: 1819. 8vo. *Full calf, neat, maps.* 1.00

VERSTEGAN, Richard. A Restitution of Decayed Intelligence in Antiquities. Concerning the most noble and renovvned English Nation. By the studie and trauaile of R. V. Antvverp: 1605. 4to. *New, full calf.* 3.00

Original edition of this scarce and much admired work. The plates in this edition are much superior to those in later ones, being exceedingly brilliant and bright impressions, and more of them.

WELWOOD, James, M. D. Memoirs of the most material Transactions in England for the last Hundred Years preceding the Revolution of 1688. London: 1700. 8vo. *Good copy, full calf.* 1.25

DODDINGTON, Geo. Bubb. Diary from March 8, 1748–9, to Feb. 6, 1761. London: 1784. 8vo. *Boards.* 1.00

A singular showing up of political perfidy.

ROSCOMON. Poems by the Earl of Roscomon. To which is added, an Essay on Poetry, by the Earl of Mulgrave, now Duke of Buckingham. Together with Poems by Mr. Richard Duke. London: 1717. 8vo. *Fine copy, full calf, gilt.* 1.50

HUDIBRAS, in Three Parts. Written in the time of the late Wars. Corrected and amended. With large Annotations, and a Preface. To this edition are added, Critical, Historical, and Explanatory Notes, by Zachary Gray, LL.D. 2 vols. Dublin: 1757. 8vo. *Portrait and other plates. Good edition, full calf.* 3.00

COLLINS, Arthur. The Baronetage of England; being an Historical and Genealogical Account of Baronets, from their first institution in the Reign of James I. .... With their Coats of Arms and Crests engraved and blazoned. 2 vols. London: 1720. 8vo. *Fine condition, full calf.* 3.00

HALL, James (Judge). Letters from the West, containing Sketches of Scenery, Manners, and Customs, and Anecdotes connected with the first settlement of the Western Sections of the United States. London: 1828. 8vo. *Boards.* 1.50

CREECH, Thomas. T. Lucretius Carus, of the Nature of Things, in six books. Translated into English verse. 2 vols. Explained and illustrated with Notes and Animadversions; being a compleat system of the Epicurean Philosophy. London: 1715. 8vo. *Old brown calf, fine condition.* 2.50

RALEIGH, Walter, Sir. An Abridgement of his History of the World. In five books. .... His Premonition to Princes. The Invention of Shipping, Relation of the Action at Cadiz, and the Voyage to Guiana. By Philip Raleigh, Esquire, his only grandson. To which is added, the Author's Life, Trial, and Death. London: 1702. 8vo. *Portrait.* 2.00

WARD, Edward. Hudibras Redivivus; or, a Burlesque Poem on the Times. London: 1705. 4to. *Good copy, in old calf. A thick quarto.*

One of the rarest of famous Ned Ward's works; and, though a little vulgar for these times, it is not without much merit.

BOLLINGBROKE, Lord. A Dissertation upon Parties; in several Letters to Caleb D'Anvers, Esq. 7th edition. London: 1749. 8vo. *Frontispiece. Good copy.* 1.00

CHRONICLES OF ENGLAND; a Metrical History. By George Raymond. London: 1842. 8vo. *Cloth. Fine portrait of Queen Elizabeth.* 1.00

A creditable performance. Extensive and valuable notes. Splendidly printed.

SALMON, Thomas. The Chronological Historian; .... from the invasion of the Romans to the 14th year of George II. 2 vols. 3d edition. With Effigies of all our English Monarchs, curiously engraven from original paintings, by Mr. Vertue. London: 1747. 8vo. 2.50

One of the most useful, clear, and concise works of the kind ever published.

BARROW, John, Esq., F. R. S. Memoirs of the Naval Worthies of Queen Elizabeth's Reign..... London: 1845. 8vo. 1.50

Thick octavo, executed in Murray's best style.

HAKLUYT, Richard. Divers Voyages touching the Discovery of America and the Islands adjacent. Edited with Notes and an Introduction, by John Winter Jones, of the British Museum. London: 1850. 8vo. *Cloth.* 3.00

COLUMBUS. Select Letters of Christopher Columbus, with other Original Documents relative to his Four Voyages to the New World. Translated and edited by R. H. Major, Esq., of the British Museum. London: 1847. 8vo. *Cloth.* 2.50

KIMBER, Isaac. The Life of Oliver Cromwell, Lord Protector of the Commonwealth of England, Scotland, and Ireland..... 4th edition. London: 1741. *Fine portrait. Very fresh copy.* 1.50

A judicious and well-written life of the noble Cromwell.

WINSTANLEY, William. The Lives of the most famous English Poets..... From the time of William the Conqueror to the reign of his present Majesty, King James II. London: 1687. 12mo. *Frontispiece. Good copy. Calf, gilt.* 1.25

MONTAGUE, Mary Wortley. The Works of the Right Honorable Lady .... including her Correspondence, Poems, and Essays..... 5 vols. London: 1803. 12mo. *Splendid portrait. Boards.* 2.25

NICOLAS, Nicholas Harris, Esq. A Synopsis of the Peerage of England; exhibiting, under alphabetical arrangement, the Date of Creation, Descent, and Present State of every Title of Peerage which has existed in this Country since the Conquest. 2 vols. London: 1825. 12mo. *Cloth backs.* 2.50

One of the most useful manuals extant.

RAY, James. A Compleat History of the Rebellion, from its first rise, in 1745, to its total suppression at the glorious Battle of Culloden, in April, 1746. .... London: 1754. 12mo. *Plates.* 1.25

RESULT OF SOME RESEARCHES among the British Archives for information relative to the Founders of New England: made in the years 1858–9–60. By Samuel G. Drake. Boston: 1860. 4to. *Cloth, extra. Map of New England, 1625. Copies of ancient portraits of Sir Francis Drake and Capt. John Smith.* 3.00
The same, *paper covers, without portraits.* 2.50

This work contains lists of all the early emigrants to New England, St. Christophers, Barbadoes, &c., which have yet been discovered.

DUMMER, Jer. A Defence of the New England Charters. London: [no date.] 8vo. *Half Morocco, neat and clean copy.* 3.00

PENHALLOW, Samuel. The History of the Wars of New England with the Eastern Indians..... *Very neatly reprinted, in 4to, by William Dodge. Full cloth.* 1.50

ANGLORUM SPECULUM, or the Worthies of England, in Church and State. .... Wherein are illustrated the Lives and Characters of the most eminent Persons since the Conquest to this present age. London: 1684. 8vo. 2.00

Thick octavo. Chiefly taken from Fuller's English Worthies, with many valuable additions.

OGILBY. The Works of Publius Virgilius Maro. Translated, adorned with Sculptures, and illustrated with Annotations. By John Ogilby, Esq., His Majesty's Cosmographer, and Geographic Printer. 3d edition. London: 1675. 8vo. *Old calf, good condition.* 2.00

Numerous whole-page copper plates.

SHELVOCKE, George, Capt. A Voyage Round the World, by way of the Great South Sea, performed in the years 1719, 20, 21, 22, in the Speedwell, of London, of 24 guns and 100 men..... London: 1726. 8vo. *Map and plates.* 1.50

SHEBBEARE, John. A Fourth Letter to the People of England on the Conduct of Ministers in Alliances, Fleets, and Armies, since the first differences on the Ohio..... London: 1756. 8vo. *Half Morocco, neat.* .75

WINSTANLEY, William. Select Lives of England's Worthies. London: 1660. 12mo. *Half Russia, neat. Few leaves wanting at beginning and end.* 1.00

Contains many things not in the later edition.

WOTTON, William, B. D. Reflections upon Ancient and Modern Learning. 2d edition, with large additions. With Dissertations upon the Epistles of Socrates, Esop's Fables, &c. By Dr Bentley. London: 1697. 8vo. *Old calf. Fine copy.* 1.25

WOODS, John. Two Years Residence in the Settlement on the English Prairie, in the Illinois Country, United States. London: 1822. 8vo. *Maps. Boards.* 1.50

WARD, Edward. The Wooden World Dissected: in the Character of a Ship of War; as also, the Characters of all the Officers..... 7th edition. London: 1760. 8vo. *Half calf, neat.* 1 00

LEYCESTER'S GHOST. 1641. 4to. [In the same volume,]
" COMMONWEALTH: conceived, spoken, and pvblished with most earnest protestation of all dutifull good will and affection towards this Realm..... [London:] 1641. 4to. *Half binding.* 1.50

Most singular productions. The latter by the Jesuit, Robert Parsons. The "Ghost" is an enigmatical poem; and not without merit.

BRIDGMAN, John. An Historical and Topographical Sketch of Knole, in Kent; with a Genealogy of the Sackville Family. Numerous engravings. 2d edition. London: 1821. 8vo. *Boards.* 1.00

SINGER, Samuel Weller. The Text of Shakespeare Vindicated from the Interpolations and Corruptions advocated by John Payne Collier, Esq. .... London: 1853. 8vo. *Cloth.* 1.50

WALLER, Edmond, Esq. Poems, &c., written upon several occasions. .... 8th edition, with additions. To which is prefixed the Author's Life. London: 1711. 8vo. *Fine copy, calf. Brilliant portrait.* 1.25

DUNTON, John. Sir Thomas Double at Court, and in High Preferments. In Two Dialogues between Sir Thomas Double and Sir Richard Comeover, alias* Mr. Whiglove, on the 27th of Sept. 1710. London: 1710. 12mo. *Calf, gilt.* 1.00

DIXON, George, Capt. A Voyage Round the World; but more particularly to the North West Coast of America in 1785-6-7-8. 2d edition. London: 1789. 4to. *Boards. Maps and plates.* 2.00

PAGES, Monsieur de. Travels Round the World, in the years 1767-8-9-70-1. Translated from the French. 2d edition. 3 vols. London: 1793. 8vo. *Bound.* 1.50

BLOME. Richard. Britannia, or, a Geographical Description of the Kingdoms of England, Scotland, and Ireland, with the Isles and Territories thereto belonging. .... Also, lists of the Names, Titles, and Seats of the Nobility and Gentry. Illustrated with a Map of each County, and 820 *Coats of Arms of patrons of the work from copper plates.* London: 1673. Folio. 5.00

PRINCE, John, (*Vicar of Berry-Pomeroy.*) Danmonii Orientales Illustres; or, the Worthies of Devon. A work, wherein the Lives and Fortunes of the most famous Divines, Statesmen, Swordsmen, Writers, [&c.] natives of that most noble Province, from before the Norman Conquest down to the present age, are Memorized, [&c] A new edition, with Notes. London: 1810. 4to. pp. 796. *A beautiful copy, in full green Turkey.* 14.00

Few books are oftener referred to by genealogists than "Prince's Worthies,"—for it is a mine of exceeding richness and of the highest authority. It was first published in 1702, in large folio form, and it was reprinted fifty years ago. This copy is one of the last impression, and besides many corrections, it is greatly enriched by the valuable notes of several learned Devonshire antiquaries. Seven fine portraits were engraved expressly for this edition; and *this* copy contains a number of highly appropriate plates, in addition to the above.

McKENNEY, Thomas L. Sketches of a Tour to the Lakes, of the Character and Customs of the Chippewa Indians. .... Baltimore: 1827. 8vo. *Plates. Half cloth, uncut.* 2.00

AUSTIN, Benjamin, Jr. Constitutional Republicanism, in opposition to Fallacious Federalism; as published occasionally in the Independent Chronicle under the signature of Old South. Boston: 1803. 8vo. *Boards.* 1.50

A MEMOIR OF THE REV. COTTON MATHER, D. D., with a Genealogy of the Family of Mather, and Portraits of Cotton and Increase Mather. By S. G. Drake. Boston: 1851. 8vo, *Full cloth, lettered.* .50

A REVIEW OF WINTHROP'S JOURNAL, as edited and published by the Hon. James Savage. By the Editor of the N. E. Historical and Gen. Register. Boston: 1854. 8vo. *Illustrated with five portraits. Full cloth.*
[In the same volume,]
AN ADDRESS delivered at the Annual Meeting of the New Eng. Historical and Genealogical Society, Jan. 20, 1858. By S. G. Drake. .75

SOME MEMOIRS OF THE REV. THOMAS PRINCE, together with a Pedigree of his Family. By S. G. Drake. Boston: 1851. 8vo. *Full cloth, lettered. Two portraits.* .50

DISCOVERY OF SOME MATERIALS for the Early History of Dorchester. .... By. S. G. Drake. Boston: 1851. 8vo. *Full cloth, lettered. Map, and two portraits.* .50

HISTORY AND ANTIQUITIES OF BOSTON, with an Introductory History of New England. By S. G. Drake. Boston: 1856. Royal 8vo. *With about 300 engravings, and 840 pages. Half calf or goat.* 5.00
The same, *cloth.* 4.50

NEW ENGLAND HISTORICAL AND GENEALOGICAL REGISTER.
14 volumes—1847 to 1860, inclusive. 8vo. *Half calf, antique.* 38.50
The same, *full cloth, gilt.* 33.25
The same, *in numbers.* 28.00

PRINCE'S NEW ENGLAND CHRONOLOGY. New edition, with addition of Memoir and Pedigree. *Twelve illustrations. Half Turkey, antique.* 5.00

HUBBARD'S HISTORY OF NEW ENGLAND. With eight steel portraits. New edition. Boston: 1848. *Half Turkey.* 3.50

WILLIAMS, Samuel, LL.D. The Natural and Civil History of Vermont. Walpole, N. H.: 1794. 8vo. *Map.* 2.00

DWIGHT, Timothy, S. T. D., LL.D. Travels in New England and New York. In 4 vols. *Maps.* London: 1823. 8vo. *Boards.* 5.50

CAMPBELL, John. Lives of the British Admirals, containing a new and accurate Naval History from the earliest periods. With continuation by Dr. Berkenhout. *With Maps.* 4 vols. London: 1781. 8vo. 3.50

CHAMBERLAYNE, Edward, LL.D., &c. Angliæ Notitia; or the Present State of England. London: 1673. 1.50

DRAKE, Roger, M. D. Sacred Chronology, drawn by Scripture evidence along that vast body of time. .... London: 1648. 4to. 2.00

www.ingramcontent.com/pod-product-compliance
Lightning Source LLC
Chambersburg PA
CBHW071436160426
43195CB00013B/1931